2ω

TWENTIETH-CENTURY WOMEN POLITICAL LEADERS

TWENTIETH-CENTURY WOMEN POLITICAL LEADERS

Claire Price-Groff

☑® Facts On File, Inc.

Twentieth-Century Women Political Leaders

Facts On File, Inc.
11 Penn Plaza
New York NY 10001

Library of Congress Cataloging-in-Publication Data

Price-Groff, Claire.
    Twentieth-century women political leaders / by Claire Price-Groff.
        p.   cm.—(Global profiles)
    Includes bibliographical references and index.
    Summary: Presents biographies of twelve women who have held positions of
political leadership around the world, including Golda Meir, Margaret Thatcher,
Winnie Mandela, Corazon Aquino, Wilma Mankiller, and Benazir Bhutto.
    ISBN 0-8160-3672-1
    1. Women politicians—Biography—Juvenile literature. [1. Women politi-
cians. 2. Politicians. 3. Women in politics. 4. Women—Biography.] I. Title. II.
Series.
HQ1236.P75 1998
305.43'329'0922—dc21   97-32373

Facts On File books are available at special discounts when purchased in bulk
quantities for businesses, associations, institutions or sales promotions.
Please call our Special Sales Department in New York at (212) 967-8800 or
(800) 322-8755.

You can find Facts On File on the World Wide Web at http://www.factsonfile.com

Text design by Cathy Rincon
Layout by Robert Yaffe
Cover design by Nora Wertz
Map on page x by Dale Williams

Printed in the United States of America

MP FOF 10 9 8 7 6 5 4 3 2 1

This book is printed on acid-free paper.

To Howard

Contents

Acknowledgments

I would like to thank all the people who helped to make this book possible—my husband Howard for his patient reading and rereadings of my rough copy, the librarians and staff at the North County Branch of the Palm Beach County Library who helped me track down resource material I needed, and the members of my critique groups who helped me polish my rough drafts into their final form.

I owe a special thank you to Judith Reifen-Ronen from the Golda Meir Memorial Association, Tel Aviv, Israel; Corazon Aquino; Sandra Parham, Texas Southern University; Sammy Still, Cherokee Nation photographer; Larry Dohrs; Leslie Kean; and everyone else who so graciously provided me with photographs. And a very special thank you to Professor Belinda Aquino, Professor of Political Science and Director of the Center for Philippine Studies, Manoa, Honolulu, for her insights into the Philippines. Also, a special thank you to Zarni of the Free Burma Coalition, whose e-mail messages kept me up to date on Aung San Suu Kyi.

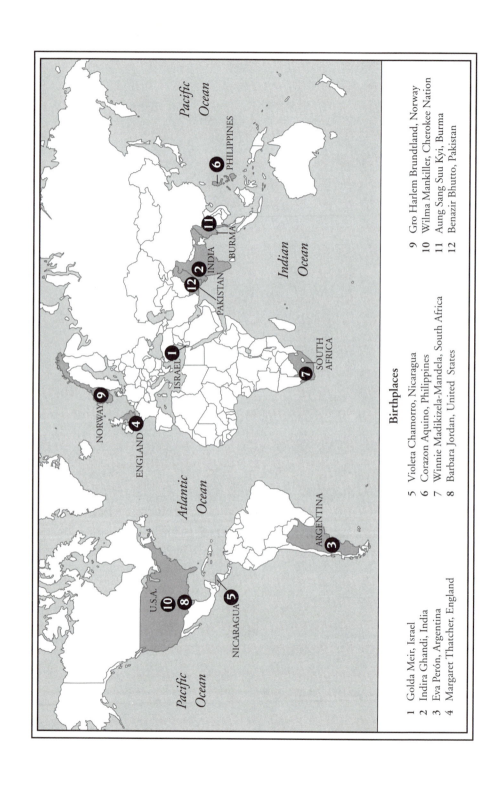

Birthplaces

1 Golda Meir, Israel
2 Indira Ghandi, India
3 Eva Perón, Argentina
4 Margaret Thatcher, England

5 Violeta Chamorro, Nicaragua
6 Corazon Aquino, Philippines
7 Winnie Madikizela-Mandela, South Africa
8 Barbara Jordan, United States

9   Gro Harlem Brundtland, Norway
10 Wilma Mankiller, Cherokee Nation
11 Aung Sang Suu Kyi, Burma
12 Benazir Bhutto, Pakistan

Introduction

Women political leaders are not a phenomenon of the 20th century. In the ancient world and throughout the Middle Ages and the Renaissance, women rulers such as Cleopatra of Egypt, Catherine de Médici of France, Elizabeth I of England, Isabella of Spain, and Catherine the Great of Russia were strong leaders who guided their countries to positions of world power. But in the past, as in the present, women leaders were the exception rather than the rule.

Throughout history, women were excluded both by law and custom from active participation in affairs of state. This did not start to change until the beginning of the 20th century, when women around the world demanded the right to vote. It has taken more than 100 years, but as the 20th century draws to a close, women have achieved political rights in nearly every country of the world.

Once women secured the right to vote, it wasn't long before they ran for and were elected to various local legislative bodies. As the number of women in politics grew, and as they gained experience, they began moving up to positions of national importance.

This book profiles 12 women who have held positions of political leadership in the second half of the 20th century.

Seven were prime ministers or presidents; one was a United States congresswoman; and one was an American Indian chief. Three of the women never actually held formal office, but are included because they were definitely political leaders and, as such, wielded tremendous power and influence in their countries.

The women in this book represent many different nations and cultures. Each of them was the first woman in her state or country to attain the position she held, opening the way for others to follow. They attained their positions through many different paths. Only a few of them chose politics as their primary career. Some women, particularly those in Asian countries, were members of families long involved in politics. Indira Gandhi, Benazir Bhutto, and Aung San Suu Kyi all were daughters of political leaders. Gandhi and Bhutto grew up surrounded by the political activities of their parents, and both were groomed for political leadership from early childhood. When her father was killed, Bhutto felt it was her obligation to carry on what he had begun. Aung San Suu Kyi's story is a bit different. Her father was killed when she was a baby, and although her mother was involved in politics, Suu Kyi did not plan to follow the family tradition. She became involved many years later when, after living in the West for most of her life, she returned home to visit her mother. She was then caught up in a growing protest movement against the military dictatorship that had ruled Burma since the 1960s.

Corazon Aquino and Violeta Chamorro were married to men who dedicated their lives to freeing their countries from repressive dictatorships. Both women's husbands were assassinated, and although neither woman had ever been active before in politics, after her husband's death, she took up her husband's mission.

Winnie Madikizela-Mandela's husband, Nelson, was not assassinated, but he was imprisoned for more than 30 years.

During that time Winnie rose to a position of leadership from which she eventually helped to free Nelson and to bring an end to South Africa's legal separation of races, known as apartheid.

Another woman who rose to power through her husband was Eva Duarte Perón, the wife of Argentina's president Juan Perón. Although she never held any official political office, Eva took an active role in her husband's administration and in her own right effected many changes in her country.

Golda Meir, one of the first women to be elected as prime minister of a modern country, had no family or political connections. She entered politics as a result of her lifelong dedication to Zionism and establishment of a free homeland for the Jewish people.

Gro Harlem Brundtland, though she did come from a politically involved family, had no particular political ambitions herself. She was a doctor dedicated to helping to improve public health conditions in her country and only entered politics when she was invited into the cabinet as a spokeswoman in that capacity. Her leadership qualities compelled her to continually increase her involvement until she was elected prime minister, not once, but three times.

Wilma Mankiller never thought of herself as a politician. In fact, Mankiller lived a life totally outside of politics until she was reawakened to her Native American heritage. Her rise to chief of the Cherokee people came only after years of increasing involvement in the plight of her people.

Because politics had traditionally been the province of men, until recently few women chose politics as their primary career goal. But this is changing. More women are choosing politics as their profession. The numbers of women in higher legislative bodies are increasing, and people throughout the world are becoming accustomed to women as leaders. Two of the women in this book have helped to set precedents for women as career politicians—Margaret Thatcher, former prime minister of the United Kingdom, and Barbara Jordan, former congresswoman from Texas.

It is ironic that while several women been elected as heads of state of Asian and European countries, there has yet to be a truly serious bid by a woman for president in the United States. Long before women had voting rights, Victoria Woodhull ran for president in 1870 but was not taken seriously. Shirley Chisholm, a black woman, ran for president in 1973, but again few took her seriously. Geraldine Ferraro, who ran as democratic vice presidential candidate in 1984, has thus far been the most serious contender. However, in the past few years several women have been elected as senators, governors, and congresswomen. Others have been appointed as presidential cabinet members and supreme court judges. Most recently, in 1997, Madeleine Albright was appointed secretary of state. Surely, it will not be too far in the future when a woman will be elected as president or vice president of the United States.

Are women different from men as leaders? Some political analysts say women are more likely to seek solutions to domestic problems through mediation and cooperation rather than through threats and confrontation. Some feel that they are more likely to seek peaceful solutions to international problems than they are to declare war. Corazon Aquino and Violeta Chamorro brought an end to the violence in their countries through their insistence on cooperation rather than confrontation with those who disagreed with them. Barbara Jordan felt that the way to improve racial relations in the United States was to work with, not against, each other. And Aung San Suu Kyi has tried to bring about change in Burma through nonviolent protest and a consistent call for peaceful negotiations between opposing parties. But Margaret Thatcher, Indira Gandhi, and Golda Meir were among the most confrontational leaders in their countries' histories.

Many people have looked to women in positions of power to take the lead in addressing family and women's concerns. And while some have, notably Gro Harlem Brundtland of Norway, most have not. Rather, Margaret Thatcher and Indira Gandhi were avowedly nonfeminist in their views, and made little effort to include other women in their administrations.

Yet in spite of their many differences, these women share certain traits. They have all demonstrated a strong sense of self and belief in their own abilities. They are ambitious, show a high degree of perseverance, and are totally dedicated to what they wish to accomplish. Many, but not all, of these women, come from families of wealth, position, and power. Nearly all of them stress that as young girls they were lucky to have families who taught them that girls were just as capable as boys of achieving any goals they set for themselves. Many of them attribute much of their strength to a firm religious faith.

Laura Liswood, who interviewed 15 women heads of state for her book *Women World Leaders* found that many of them said they had to work harder to achieve and maintain their positions than a man would have had to do. Several of the women Liswood interviewed said they resented the fact that when the media wrote about male political leaders, they stressed their leadership styles, but that when they wrote about women political leaders, they were more apt to write about their dress and hair styles.

Some of the women said that being women did present them with special problems. Corazon Aquino and Benazir Bhutto both have said that because, as women, they were brought up to be polite and accommodating, it was difficult for them to learn how to give orders instead of asking for compliance.

Asked what advice they would pass on to other women aspiring to political leadership, the women profiled in this book and other women leaders said it is important to have a strong belief in what you wish to accomplish, to have specific goals, and to never let anyone dissuade you from those goals. Others stressed the importance of having a group of trusted advisers who are honest and have a high degree of integrity. Corazon Aquino said she learned that while these qualities in her advisers were essential, what was even more important was having a group of people who were able to work well together. Benazir Bhutto said that while a leader must be flexible, she must never abandon her basic principles.

Politics is ever changing. When I began writing this book, several of the women discussed were currently holding office. Since that time, most of their terms of office have ended. As I finish the book, there are fewer women in positions of high political office than there were when I began it. But the precedents have been set and the numbers of women political leaders will grow.

There have been—and are—many other women political leaders not included in this book. Their exclusion does not imply that they are less important than the women who are profiled here, but simply that the scope of this book did not allow their inclusion.

These women include:

- Sirimavo Bandaranaike, prime minister of Sri Lanka, 1960–65, 1970–77, and 1994–
- Elizabeth Domitien, prime minister of Central African Republic, 1975–76
- Maria de Lurdes Pintassilgo, prime minister of Portugal, 1979–80
- Mary Eugenia Charles, prime minister of Dominica, 1980–95
- Milka Planinc, prime minister of Yugoslavia, 1982–86
- Kazimiera Prunskiene, prime minister of Lithuania, 1990–91
- Khaleda Zia, prime minister of Bangladesh, 1991–96
- Edith Cresson, prime minister of France, 1991–92

- Hanna Suchocka, prime minister of Poland, 1992–93
- Kim Campbell, prime minister of Canada, 1993
- Tansu Ciller, prime minister of Turkey, 1993–96
- Sylvie Kinigi, prime minister of Burundi, 1993–94
- Agathe Uwilingiyimana, prime minister of Rwanda, 1993–94
- Reneta Indjova, prime minister of Bulgaria, 1994–95
- Claudette Werleigh, prime minister of Haiti, 1995–96
- Sheik Hasina Wajed, prime minister of Bangladesh 1996–
- Janet Jagan, prime minister of Guyana, 1997–
- Vigdis Finnbogadóttir, president of Iceland, 1980–96
- Agatha Barbara, president of Malta, 1982–87
- Mary Robinson, president of Ireland, 1990–
- Sabine Bergmann-Pohl, president of the Parliament of German Democratic Republic, 1990
- Chandrika Kumaratunga, president of Sri Lanka 1994–

Unlike in past generations, a young woman of the 21st century who wishes to make politics her career, can aspire to becoming a prime minister or a president of her country.

Further Reading

Liswood, Laura A., *Women World Leaders: Fifteen Great Politicians Tell Their Stories*. London: Pandora Press, 1995. Contains profiles and interviews with several of the women in this book.

Brill, Alida. Ed. *A Rising Public Voice: Women in Politics Worldwide*. New York: The Feminist Press, 1995. An excellent examination of women in politics with profiles, essays, and statistics.

Golda Meir, Israel's fourth prime minister, saw her dream of a new home-land for the Jewish people come true. But she knew the establishment of the state was only the beginning of a long struggle for peace with its Arab neighbors. She once said, "Our generation reclaimed the land, our children fought the war—and our grandchildren should enjoy the peace." Israel became a nation in 1948. Fifty years later, in 1998, that peace is yet to be realized. (Courtesy Golda Meir Memorial Association, Tel Aviv, Israel)

Golda Meir of Israel

(1898–1978)

In 1909, an ad in the local newspaper invited everyone in the neighborhood to attend a special meeting arranged by the Young Sisters Society, a small group of fourth-grade girls from Milwaukee's Fourth Street Elementary School.

On the night of the meeting, eleven-year-old Golda Mabovitch peeked out from backstage and watched her little sister recite the poem that she had memorized for the occasion. Golda had worked hard organizing this night. She had placed the advertisement, rented the auditorium, sent out personal invitations, and planned the program.

When the poem ended, the audience applauded. Golda's turn was next. Golda didn't recite a poem or sing a song or do a dance. She stood alone on the stage, looked out at the adults who filled the hall, and explained why she had called the meeting. She told them that though public school was free, parents were expected to purchase the textbooks their children needed. Golda reminded her audience that many of the students and their families were recent immigrants who simply could not afford to purchase books—and that as a

1

result, those students were falling behind in their classes. Golda didn't think this was fair and she asked for donations to help purchase more textbooks. She was convincing; at the end of the evening enough money had been collected so every child in school had the textbooks he or she needed.

Golda would spend the rest of her life working hard for causes in which she believed. When she grew up, that cause became Zionism, a movement to establish a free homeland for the Jewish people. But Golda never dreamed she would one day be Israel's prime minister.

Golda was born May 3, 1898, in Kiev, Russia, the middle daughter of Blume and Moshe Mabovitch. Life in Russia was hard, especially for Jewish people, who were often the victims of widespread anti-Semitism (discrimination against Jews). As a little girl, Golda hid in terror as she watched her father hammer boards across the door of their home trying to protect his family from *pogroms*, periodic raids against Jewish villages conducted by the czar's soldiers.

Golda's parents wanted to emigrate to America, where they could live free from this kind of persecution. When Golda was four years old, her father sailed to America and settled in Milwaukee, Wisconsin. By 1906, he had saved enough money to send for his family. But getting to America for Golda, her mother, and her sisters was not easy. First they had to make their way overland to the seaport. Then came the long trip across the ocean. When they finally arrived in New York, there was another long journey on a train to Milwaukee.

Golda was thrilled with the house that her father had rented for the family. It contained wonders such as an icebox,

running water, and even a flush toilet in the backyard outhouse. The house was so large that Blume Mabovitch opened
a grocery store in the front rooms. Golda's job was to open
the store each day, even though this made her late for school.
Despite her chronic tardiness, she did well in her classes and
looked forward to completing high school and even going to
college.

But her parents had other plans for her. They thought
it was more important for a young girl to marry than to
attend high school. Following the custom of the old country, they arranged a match for Golda soon after her 14th
birthday. Golda was determined not to marry this boy. She
wrote to her older sister Shayna, who lived in Denver,
asking her to help. Shayna invited Golda to come to
Denver to live with her and finish school. She sent Golda
money, but not quite enough for the train fare. To earn the
difference, Golda taught English to new immigrants for
10 cents an hour. When she saved what she needed, she
told her parents she was staying at a friend's house but
instead took a train to Denver.

In Denver, Golda met Shayna's friends, many of whom
were Zionists, a group dedicated to establishing a new
homeland for Jews in Palestine, where they could live free
from the persecution they suffered in Russia and other
European countries. Golda sat in on the meetings and soon
became a Zionist herself.

Shayna felt responsible for her little sister. She told Golda
what she could and could not do, much like a mother would.
But Golda was a self-willed and stubborn young woman. She
resented Shayna's rules, and the two sisters often argued.
Finally, Golda moved out of her sister's apartment and rented
one of her own. To support herself, she dropped out of school
and went to work in a curtain factory. When her father
learned that Golda was no longer living with her sister, he

told her if she came home, he would allow her to go back to school.

Golda did return home, graduated from high school, and went on to teacher's college. She also became active in Poale Zion, a local Zionist organization. She had become so dedicated to Zionism that instead of seeking a teaching job when she finished college, she worked for Poale Zion. Part of her job was making speeches on street corners, recruiting new members, and asking for donations. Golda's father thought this behavior was disgraceful for a young woman. He threatened to follow her and drag her home by her braids. He did follow her but was so impressed with her earnestness and passion when she spoke that he never again said anything against what she was doing.

While she had been in Denver, Golda had begun dating Morris Meyerson, whom she had met at a Zionist meeting. Later, Morris came to Milwaukee to ask her to marry him. Golda wanted to emigrate to Palestine and live on a kibbutz, a communal farm where members share work, tools, land, and money. She told Morris she would marry him if he would come with her. He agreed, and they were married in 1917.

In 1921, Golda and Morris emigrated to Palestine and joined the Merhavia Kibbutz. At first, the people in charge thought that people from an American city would be unable to adapt to the hard farm and field work they would be expected to do. But Meyerson soon proved herself to be a valuable member. Though she had never worked on a farm before, when she was assigned to work in the chicken house, she improved egg production. And later, working in the kitchen, she introduced new items to the menu as well as little luxuries such as tablecloths and flowers for Sabbath dinners.

While Golda was happy at the kibbutz, Morris hated it, so they left. They moved to Tel Aviv, where Morris found a job as a bookkeeper and Golda worked for Histadrut, an organization that coordinated labor and social services for the growing number of Jewish pioneers. In 1924, Golda gave birth to her son Menachem. When the baby was a few months old, Golda left Morris to return to Merhavia, but because she did not want to break up her marriage, she later rejoined her husband.

This time the family settled in Jerusalem. Soon, their daughter Sarah was born. To supplement the family income, Golda took in laundry. These were not happy years for her. She hadn't come to Palestine to wipe noses and change diapers; she sought to build a new homeland.

She got her chance in 1928 when she was offered a position as a secretary for Histadrut. But then a few years later, her daughter Sarah contracted a serious kidney disease and Meyerson took her to the United States where she could obtain the best medical treatment. For the next two years, while Sarah was being treated, Meyerson worked for Pioneer Women, an American Zionist organization. She traveled throughout the country raising money and recruiting new pioneers to emigrate to Palestine. When Sarah regained her health, Meyerson brought her home to Palestine. Meyerson resumed her work for Histadrut, this time as a member of their Executive Committee. By 1936 she had become head of the political department of the Histadrut.

"From my early youth I believed in two things: one, the need for Jewish sovereignty, so that Jews . . . can be master of their own fate; and two, a society based on justice and equality without exploitation. But I was never so naive or foolish as to think that if you merely believe in something it happens. You must struggle for it."

—Golda Meir

By the end of the 1930s, a new German leader, Adolf Hitler, had come to power. Hitler's armies had conquered several European countries. One of Hitler's aims was to rid Europe of all Jews, and in each country he took over, Jews were sent to concentration camps where many of them were gassed or worked to death. In 1939 Meyerson was a delegate to an international meeting on the "Jewish Problem." Everyone agreed that Jewish people in middle and eastern Europe were in grave danger, but not one country agreed to allow Jewish immigrants into their country. Britain, which at the time ruled Palestine, had earlier supported the idea of a Jewish homeland in Palestine. But during World War II, under pressure from Palestine's Arabs, they changed their minds and issued the White Paper, a document that placed strict limits on the number of Jews allowed to enter Palestine. Knowing the dangers European Jews faced, Meyerson defied the law and helped to smuggle Jewish refugees into Palestine.

Golda Meyerson signing Israel's Declaration of Independence, May 14, 1948
(Courtesy Golda Meir Memorial Association, Tel Aviv, Israel)

When the war ended, more than 6 million Jews had been murdered. Those who managed to survive had nowhere to go. Many came to the United States, but others wanted to go to Palestine. Britain's White Paper prevented this. Those who tried to get to Palestine were held in displaced persons camps. Meanwhile, Meyerson, along with David Ben-Gurion and other Jewish leaders led the movement to make Israel an independent nation. During this time, Meyerson once again defied the law and smuggled refugees into Palestine.

In 1946, when the British arrested most of the Zionist leaders who were pushing for independence, Meyerson was appointed acting head of the Jewish Agency, making her the leader of the most powerful Jewish group in Palestine.

In January 1947, the question of whether to make Israel independent was turned over to the United Nations. Finally, in November of that year, the decision came. Palestine would be divided into two states—one Jewish and one Arab. On May 14, 1948, the world watched as Meyerson, with tears streaming down her face, added her name to those who signed Israel's Declaration of Independence. As momentous an event as it was, there was no time to rejoice.

Within hours of the signing, Egyptian bombs exploded over the Israeli city of Tel Aviv. Israel had been attacked by seven Arab nations that vowed to push the fledgling country into the sea. Meyerson traveled to the United States to raise money for the army. On her return, she was named Israel's first ambassador to the Soviet Union. Along with the rest of Israel, Meyerson rejoiced when her country defeated her Arab attackers. But that was only the first of several wars between Israel and its Arab neighbors.

From 1949 to 1956, Meyerson served as Israel's minister of labor. When Israel became a state, the government declared a policy of unlimited immigration for Jews from anywhere in the world. This brought a tremendous influx of immigrants to the new country from all parts of the world. As minister of labor, Meyerson was in charge of overseeing the building of new housing and establishing job training for the new immigrants.

In 1956, Israeli government officials dropped their European names and took Hebrew ones—Golda Meyerson became Golda Meir ("to illuminate"). From 1956 to 1966 Meir was foreign minister. By 1966, Meir had worked for her country for more than 40 years. She had never taken a vacation or a day off, except for several times when she was hospitalized for various illnesses. When she was 66 years old, she said she had had enough and announced her retirement. She left her government post but remained active in politics and was drafted to head the Mapai Party (later the Labor Party).

In 1969, at the age of 70, Meir was elected as prime minister. During her tenure, she dealt with domestic problems such as building new housing and finding jobs for the continuing influx of new immigrants. She also had to contend with increasing terrorist bombings and the constant threat of war from Israel's Arab neighbors. She held meetings with Jordan's King Hussein in an attempt to negotiate a peace, but also met with President Richard Nixon of the United States to request aid and arms so Israel would be prepared for war if it came.

"The only alternative to war is peace and the only road to peace is negotiations."

—Golda Meir

Meir often held cabinet meetings at her home at night to discuss important state matters, but only after she served her homemade chicken soup. Meir looked like everyone's idea of a kindly old grandmother, but she was a strong leader who never compromised her ideals. She abhorred war and wept openly over both Israeli and Arab casualties, yet she consistently sent the army into battle and always ordered retaliatory action against Arab terrorist attacks. She was condemned many times by the United Nations for this, but she asserted that Israel had no alternative but to defend itself.

On Yom Kippur Day, 1973, Israel was once again attacked by several Arab nations. Meir had been warned of the attack but hadn't mobilized the army because she didn't think the Arabs would violate this holiest of all Jewish holidays. Also, she did not want to be the first to strike. Thus, when the attack came, Israel suffered heavy losses. Though Israel went on to win this war, many people could not forgive Meir's misjudgment and she was forced to resign as prime minister in April 1974.

Though no longer an official part of Israel's government, she remained active and outspoken until her death on December 8, 1978. When she died, it was revealed that she had been fighting leukemia for the past 12 years.

Golda Meir lived to see her dream of a free Jewish homeland, but unfortunately, she did not live to see the peace she hoped would come between Israel and its neighbors. She remains for Israel and for the world a symbol of strength and dedication to the dream of freedom. A *New York Times* writer paid tribute to her with these words: "The miracle of Golda Meir was how one person could perfectly embody the spirit of so many."

Chronology

May 3, 1898	Golda Mabovitch born in Kiev, Russia
1906	emigrates to Milwaukee, Wisconsin
1915	joins Zionist group

1917	marries Morris Meyerson
1921	emigrates to Palestine, joins kibbutz
1934	is elected as secretary of Executive Commitee of Histadrut
1939–45	helps smuggle Jewish refugees into Palestine
May 14, 1948	signs Israel's Declaration of Independence
1949–56	serves as Israel's first minister of labor
1956	changes name to Golda Meir
1956–66	serves as Israel's foreign minister
1969	is elected prime minister
December 8, 1978	Golda Meir dies

Further Reading

Adler, David. *Our Golda: The Story of Golda Meir*. New York: Viking Press, 1984. For younger readers, with a focus on her childhood.

Browne, Ray B. Ed. *Contemporary Heroes and Heroines*. Detroit: Gale Research, 1990. Contains good profile of Meir.

Felder, Deborah G. *The 100 Most Influential Women of All Time*. New York: Citadel Press, 1996. Contains profile of Meir.

Gelb, Arthur and A. M. Rosenthal and Marvin Siegel. Eds. *The New York Times Great Lives of the Twentieth Century*. New York: Times Books, 1988. An excellent in-depth profile of Meir.

Gibbs, Richard. *Women Prime Ministers*. New Jersey: Silver Burdett Press, 1982. Contains good chapter on Meir. For young adults.

Keller, Mollie. *Golda Meir.* New York: Franklin Watts, 1983. A good young adult biography.

Liston, Robert A. *Women Who Ruled: Cleopatra–Elizabeth II.* New York: Julian Messner, 1978. Contains a good chapter on Meir.

McAuley, Karen. *Golda Meir.* New York: Chelsea House, 1985. A thorough young adult biography with good historical background.

Meir, Golda. *My Life.* New York: Putnam, 1975. Meir's autobiography.

Meir, Menachem. *My Mother Golda Meir.* New York: Arbor House, 1983. A personal glimpse of Golda as a mother as well as world figure.

Noble, Iris. *Israel's Golda Meir: Pioneer to Prime Minister.* New York: Julian Messner, 1974. Written at the height of Meir's career.

Indira Gandhi, who served two separate terms as prime minister of India, helped to lead her country to a premier position among the developing countries of the world. (Courtesy Embassy of India)

Indira Gandhi of India

(1917–1984)

On October 30, 1984, Indira Gandhi, prime minister of India, wrote in her diary, "If I die a violent death as some fear and a few are plotting, I know the violence will be in the thought and the action of the assassin, not in my dying . . ."

On October 31, 1984, Gandhi finished her breakfast with her grandchildren. She adjusted her sari, stepped outside, and began her morning stroll through the garden of her private residence to her office. As she approached the flower-covered gate that separated the two parts of her property, two security guards swung their guns to their shoulders and opened fire on her. Bleeding and dazed, her body twisted and she crumpled to the ground. India's prime minister was dead.

Indira Gandhi dedicated her entire life to her country. As a young child, she helped her parents lead the struggle to free India from British colonial rule. As an adult, she assisted her father, Jawaharlal Nehru, in his position as India's first prime minister. Later, she became India's third prime minister, and as such, took her place as one of the world's most powerful and respected leaders.

Indira Priyadarshini ("dear to behold") Nehru was born on November 19, 1917, in Allahabad, India. Traditionally, in Indian culture, male children are more highly valued than are female children. But this was not the case in the Nehru family. On learning of Indira's birth, her grandfather said, "this daughter of Jawaharlal . . . may prove better than a thousand sons."

When Indira was born, her parents were active participants in the Indian National Congress Party's struggle to free India from British colonial rule. They worked closely with Mohandas (Mahatma) Gandhi, the leader of India's freedom movement, who became known throughout the world for his policies of civil disobedience and nonviolent protest.

One way Gandhi and Indira's parents protested against British rule was to stop using British-made goods. When Indira was four years old, she watched her parents throw every British-made article they owned into a huge bonfire on their front lawn. For her own contribution, Indira tossed her favorite British-made doll into the flames. She had made her first sacrifice for India.

Mohandas Gandhi's policy was one of strict nonviolence. But protesting against British rule, even in a nonviolent way, was dangerous. British police and soldiers beat, clubbed, and shot protesters. They tried to prevent large public meetings and block communication between different groups of protesters. They imprisoned the Congress Party leaders such as Indira's parents.

Instead of playing normal childhood games, Indira played at protest. She would place her dolls into opposing lines of Indians and British, then have the British dolls beat the Indian ones with sticks. At other times, she would stand on a table, her arms flung wide, making impassioned speeches about a free India. When she was 12, she decided the time for play had ended. She tried to join the Indian National Congress

Party, only to be told she must wait until she was 18. But Indira wasn't one to wait. She recruited thousands of India's children and formed what she called the Monkey Brigade. The children ran errands, helped with cooking, wrapped bandages, and even acted as couriers carrying secret messages between groups of protesters.

Young Indira may have been actively involved in India's freedom movement, but at the same time she was receiving an education. For a while she attended a Roman Catholic school, but most of her schooling was at home, where she read widely in her father's well-stocked library. One time while her father was in prison, he wrote her a series of letters discussing philosophy, history, and politics. These letters became an important component of her education. In her later life, she had the letters published as a book that was used in Indian schools.

When Indira was 17 her mother, who was ill with tuberculosis, went to Switzerland for medical treatment. Indira went with her. Unfortunately the treatment was not successful and Indira's mother died. After her mother's death, Indira remained in the West and went to England to study at Oxford University.

While she was at Oxford, World War II had begun and the Germans were dropping bombs on English cities. Indira helped the war effort by driving an ambulance. While in England, she fell in love with Feroze Gandhi, an old family friend who was also studying at Oxford. (Gandhi is a common name in India —Feroze was no relation to Mohandas Gandhi.) Indira and Feroze returned to India in 1942 and announced their engagement. Indira's family belonged to India's highest social class, or caste, and her father felt that Feroze, who came from a lower caste, was not a suitable husband for Indira. But Indira persisted and her father relented. He even wove the pink sari she wore for her wedding while he, once again, was incarcerated in a British prison.

Both Feroze and Indira were active in India's freedom movement. Shortly after their arrival in India, Indira Gandhi was jailed for her protest activities. After her release from prison, she and Feroze settled into married life. They had two sons, first Rajiv, then two years later, Sanjay.

Gandhi became her father's assistant, often spending more time in his home than her own. In 1947, when India finally won its independence, Indira's father Jawaharlal Nehru was elected prime minister. Gandhi left her husband's home and moved into her father's, where she acted as his First Lady. She hosted state dinners, accompanied him on state travel, and served as his primary deputy.

In 1955, she became the first woman to sit on the Indian National Congress Party's executive committee. In 1959, she was elected as president of the party, a position once held by her grandfather and, later, her father. Some members of the party were unhappy with Gandhi as president, not because she was a woman, but because they felt she was using her father's name to advance her own career. To avoid further criticism, she refused a second term as president, saying she wanted to devote all her time to helping her father.

Jawaharlal Nehru died of a stroke in 1964. For several months, Gandhi was overcome with grief and went into a period of seclusion. When she recovered, she was appointed minister of information by Lal Bahadur Shastri, who succeeded her father as prime minister. In a country as vast as India, where millions of people lived in tiny villages far from any city, and where much of the population was illiterate, radio was the only means of providing information to them. As minister of information, Gandhi promoted the manufacture of more radios, sponsored the opening of more radio stations, and encouraged freedom of the press.

In 1966 Shastri died, and Gandhi was asked to step in as interim prime minister. The party leaders knew Gandhi would be popular with the people because of her father, and they felt they could use her to push their own agenda. They were right about her being popular. They were dead wrong about being able to manipulate her. Gandhi turned out to be a strong and determined leader who took orders from no one. She wanted to institute programs designed to alleviate the almost unendurable poverty in which millions of Indians lived. She pushed for better education. She urged private investment from foreign countries to begin to build India's industries. Asserting her independence, she refused to align India with either the United States or the Soviet Union—the two major rivals in the post–World War II cold war—but instead insisted on remaining neutral, thus receiving aid from both. She was also responsible for building India into a nuclear power by sponsoring the testing of atomic weapons and the development of nuclear power plants. Her strong stands on many issues made her popular with some factions but brought condemnation from others. Once, while she was speaking to a crowd, a dissenter threw a rock that hit her in the face and broke her nose. Gandhi stemmed the flow of blood with her sari and finished her speech.

In 1971, Gandhi was elected prime minister in her own right. She greatly increased her popularity when she led India to victory in a war with Pakistan and helped to create the new country of Bangladesh out of what had been East Pakistan.

But trouble was ahead for Gandhi. She became increasingly autocratic in pushing drastic measures in her attempts to reduce poverty and improve living conditions for millions

"We want peace because there is another war to fight—the war against poverty and ignorance. We have promises to keep with our people—of work, food, clothing, and shelter, health and education."

—Indira Gandhi

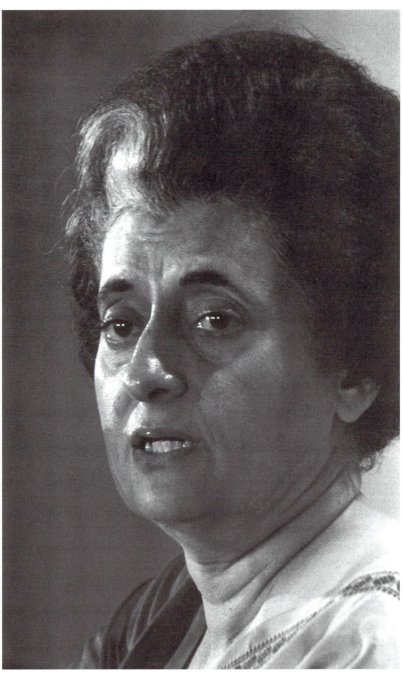

Indira Gandhi during an official visit to the United States in the early 1980s (Library of Congress)

of India's poor. Following the advice of her son Sanjay, whom she was grooming to follow in her footsteps, she introduced mandatory sterilization of women as a means of lowering the birth rate. This was a very unpopular move and Gandhi lost much of her support. She was also accused of having violated election rules in the 1971 election and was asked to resign her post as prime minister.

Instead, she declared a state of emergency. Thousands who opposed her were arrested and jailed without trial. Civil rights were suspended and strict censorship was imposed on the media. The woman who had helped to found India as the world's largest democracy had apparently become a dictator.

Gandhi claimed she had no choice. She said she was preventing the government from being taken over by those who would have ruined all she had done for India. Perhaps she was right. To the surprise of her detracters, once she felt the situation had calmed down, she called for new elections, thinking her own popularity would carry her to victory. This time it was she who was wrong. She was voted out of office in 1977. Without protest, she accepted the people's decision and stepped down.

But she did not remain in private life for long. In 1980, there was another election and Gandhi was once again elected prime minister. She rejoiced in her reelection but suffered a great personal loss at this time. Her son Sanjay was killed when the small private plane he was piloting crashed. She mourned her son but carried on with her duties.

"In India democracy has given too much license to the people. Sometimes bitter medicine has to be administered to a patient to cure him."

—Indira Gandhi

In a land of many religions and many cultures, there were always clashes and disagreements. In the early 1980s, some Sikhs, members of a small but powerful religious and political sect, wanted to break away from India and establish an independent state. Gandhi was vehemently against this. She tried to negotiate a peaceful settlement but was unable to. Tensions between the rebels and Gandhi's supporters continued to escalate. There were several incidents of violence, and many people were killed.

Finally, an armed group of Sikhs took refuge inside one of their most sacred places, the Golden Temple of Amritsar. Temples were usually considered sanctuaries safe from attack. Gandhi knew this, and she knew that she would be heavily criticized if she attacked. But when the violence continued and the rebel Sikhs killed several more people, she felt that she had no choice. In June 1984, she ordered her troops to take possession of the temple. Gandhi's troops did take the temple and subdue the rebels, but only after a fierce fight that lasted 24 hours. There were many casualties and deaths on both sides. As expected Gandhi was widely criticized for her actions, both by the Sikhs and by many other groups who felt she was wrong to send troops into any temple.

After the attack Gandhi's advisers suggested that no Sikhs be allowed to serve as personal security guards for the prime minister. Gandhi did not accept this advice because she said that she did not want to discriminate against any one group and because she felt that removing the Sikh guards would only cause more dissension. Gandhi's decision was a fatal one. On October 31, 1984—four months after the Amritsar incident—two security guards gunned down Gandhi. These guards were Sikhs who were seeking revenge for the attack on the Golden Temple.

After her assassination, Gandhi's body lay in state on a flower-covered bier as most of India mourned the death of the woman they called *Mataji*—revered mother. Her son Rajiv, who succeeded her as prime minister, led the funeral procession to the banks of the Yamuna River where, in Hindu fashion, he set fire to her funeral pyre.

Though much of Indira Gandhi's political career was fraught with controversy, she stands as one of India's greatest and most beloved figures, along with her father and Mahatma Gandhi.

Chronology

November 19, 1917	Indira Nehru born in Allahabad, India
1929	organizes children's Monkey Brigade
1936	begins Somerville College at Oxford University
1938	joins National Congress Party
March 26, 1942	marries Feroze Gandhi
1942	Indira Gandhi jailed by British
1944	son Rajiv born
1946	son Sanjay born
August 14, 1947	India becomes independent; Indira's father becomes prime minister
1959	Indira Gandhi elected president of National Congress Party
1960	Feroze Gandhi dies
1960	Indira Gandhi resigns party post to assist father full-time
1964	Indira Gandhi's father, Jawaharlal Nehru, dies
1964	Indira Gandhi appointed minister of information

1966	appointed as interim prime minister
1971	elected prime minister
1975	accused of electoral fraud; asked to resign
1975	declares state of emergency; imposes dictatorial rule
1977	holds free election and loses
1980	reelected as prime minister
June 1984	sends army troops into Golden Temple
October 31, 1984	Indira Gandhi assassinated by Sikh security guards

Further Reading

Ashby, Ruth and Deborah Gore Ohrn. Eds. *Herstory*. New York: Viking, 1995. Short, but insightful profile of Gandhi.

Browne, Ray B. Ed. *Contemporary Heroes and Heroines*. Detroit: Gale Research, 1990. Good profile of Gandhi.

Butler, Francelia. *Indira Gandhi*. New York: Chelsea House, 1986. Thoroughly researched full biography for young adults.

Commire, Anne. Ed. *Historic World Leaders: Africa, Middle East, Asia, Pacific*. Detroit: Gale Research, 1995. Excellent in-depth profile.

Currimbhoy, Nayana. *Indira Gandhi*. New York: Franklin Watts, 1985. A young adult book that examines Gandhi's controversial rule and her pivotal role in India. Good historical and political development background.

Felder, Deborah G. *The 100 Most Influential Women of All Time*. New York: Citadel Press, 1996. Short profile of Gandhi included.

Gibbs, Richard. *Women Prime Ministers*. New Jersey: Silver Burdett Press, 1982. For younger readers, but very thorough.

Haskins, James. *India Under Indira and Rajiv Gandhi*. Hillside, New Jersey: Enslow Publishers, 1989. A good young adult biography. Covers both Indira and her son who succeeded her. Examines India's political history and the Gandhis' place in it.

Liston, Robert A. *Women Who Ruled: Cleopatra–Elizabeth II.* New York: Julian Messner, 1978. Contains good profile of Gandhi.

Eva Duarte Perón took a personal interest in many of Argentina's affairs. Here she is speaking at Escuela Superior, Buenos Aires, May 31, 1951. (Courtesy Archivo General de la Nacion de la Republica Argentina)

Eva Duarte Perón of Argentina

(1919–1952)

The time is 1948. The place is Argentina. Each day hundreds of native South Americans wrapped in handwoven ponchos, shabbily dressed country farmers, and tired-looking factory workers sit crowded onto benches in the waiting room of the Ministry of Labor. Their obvious poverty contrasts sharply with the ornate decoration of the room. They wait patiently, chattering among themselves and quieting their crying children. Finally, after several hours, someone calls out, "Ya viene!" (She comes.)

Babies are hushed. Talking ceases. Everyone watches as an elegantly dressed woman strides into the hall and ascends the raised platform to her desk. Each person hopes that today he or she will be among those allowed to speak with the woman they call Lady of Hope.

A woman, her child cradled in her arms, timidly approaches the dais and sits in the chair beside the desk. She speaks softly, telling the lady about herself and her seven children, all of whom are living in a single room.

The large rings on the lady's fingers sparkle as she reaches beneath the blotter on her desk. She hands the woman two 50-peso notes. She also gives her tickets she can redeem for a new house, furniture, and a new wardrobe for her entire family. The daily parade of giving has begun.

The lady was Eva Duarte Perón, head of the Eva Perón Foundation and the wife of President Juan Domingo Perón. Although running the foundation was Eva's only official role in her husband's government, she was very much his partner in his leadership of Argentina.

Eva Perón's rise to political power was a strange one. She began life as the illegitimate daughter of a poor country woman. As a young girl, her main ambition was to become a wealthy actress and to one day get even with those people whom she felt had looked down on her and her family. But she became far more than an actress—she became the first lady of Argentina and the most influential woman in the country.

Eva Marie Ibaguren was born on May 7, 1919, in the tiny village of Los Toldos in the midst of Argentina's dusty pampas region. She was the youngest of five children born to Juana Ibaguren, who was the mistress of Juan Duarte. Although Duarte had a legal wife with whom he had legitimate children, he spent part of each week with Eva's mother and provided financial assistance for her and her children.

That Eva's family were considered social outcasts was made painfully clear to her when her father died. Señora Ibaguren took Eva and her siblings to the funeral, but they were unwelcome, and on the long walk to the cemetery they were forced to tag along behind the legitimate family and their friends. Seven-year-old Eva never forgot this humiliation. With Duarte gone, Eva's family was left penniless. They left Los Toldos and moved to Junín, another poor country town where Señora Ibaguren operated a boardinghouse. But even in the new town, Eva could not escape the shadow of her mother's shame.

Like many other young girls, Eva read movie magazines and imagined herself living the glamorous life of a movie star. At 14 she decided to make her dream a reality. Hoping to gain a measure of respectability, she adopted her father's name of Duarte as her own and eventually made her way to Buenos Aires to seek her fortune as an actress. She was not an overnight success. For seven years she found only occasional small parts, and often did not have enough to eat. She never became a film star but eventually did make a minor name for herself in the lead role in a radio series, "Heroines of History."

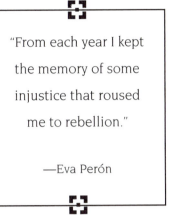

"From each year I kept the memory of some injustice that roused me to rebellion."

—Eva Perón

One night in 1943, Eva attended a political rally where she was introduced to Colonel Juan Perón, one of the leaders of a revolution that had recently overthrown the former government. Perhaps because both Perón and Eva had come from poor backgrounds and shared a hatred of the wealthy they were drawn to each other even though Perón was almost twice Eva's age.

Eva moved into Perón's apartment, where she enjoyed being part of his powerful inner circle. She sat in on political meetings, making coffee and emptying ashtrays, but refused to cook meals. When Perón asked her to prepare dinner, she brought several cans, a can opener, and a handful of forks to the table. In one of her later speeches, she said, "When a woman goes into politics, the man eats cold *puchero* [stew]."

Because Juan was very popular with the people, the other leaders of the revolution feared he was becoming too powerful. In an attempt to prevent this, they arrested him and threw him into prison. Some stories say that while Juan was in prison, Eva organized protests by making speeches to factory workers and going door to door asking for their support. This story is only one of the many legends that have grown up around Eva Perón. Eva was not the one who organized the workers, but when they heard of Juan's imprisonment, thousands of them marched through the streets demanding his freedom. Fearing a mass uprising, the military leaders freed Juan Perón. They also promised to hold an election to choose a new president to lead the new government. Juan would be one of the candidates.

To avoid being criticized for living with a woman to whom he was not married, Perón and Eva wed. Perón campaigned for her husband, making radio speeches and personal appearances. Most of her appeals were made to the masses of poor, whom she called her *descamisados* ("shirtless ones"). Her speeches were full of flowery phrases and syrupy emotion, but the people responded to them and soon Perón was as popular as her husband.

Juan Perón won the election and Eva became Argentina's first lady. Unlike most presidents' wives, she took an active part in her husband's administration, acting as one of his top aides and advisers. Both Eva and Juan admired Hitler and Mussolini, the two Fascist leaders who led Europe into World War II. So it was not surprising that although the Peróns had promised democracy, once they were in office, they had anyone who opposed them or disagreed with them imprisoned or deported. With Eva's encouragement, Juan took over all the radio stations and newspapers. It wasn't long before the Peróns had total control over the country. The more power they wielded, the more they seemed to want.

In 1947, Eva Perón made an official visit to Europe, where she was awarded a high decoration by Francisco Franco, Spain's Fascist dictator. She brought generous loans and gifts to Spain, France, and Italy, all of whose economies had been ruined during World War II, which had ended only two years before. She traveled in grand style with a privately outfitted plane and a large staff to attend to her every need. Though her trip was considered a huge success, she was disappointed that she was not received by the queen of England.

After her trip, she poured her energies into helping Argentina's poor through her Eva Perón Foundation. In addition to the gifts she distributed to the hundreds who came daily to her office, she sent truckloads of clothes and household goods throughout the country to be distributed directly to people's homes. The foundation built schools, hospitals, orphanages, and homes for the elderly and single mothers. It trained thousands of doctors, nurses, and social service workers.

Though at first privately funded by Perón, money quickly poured into the foundation from other sources. Perón asked every Argentinian to donate one day's salary. She also expected large donations from businesses and corporations. Many gave willingly, but no one dared refuse. Perón's vengeance against those who didn't cooperate was swift and harsh.

No accounts of income or expenses for the foundation were kept, but each year 400,000 pairs of shoes, 500,000 sewing machines, 200,000 cooking pots, and much more was purchased. More than 14,000 people were employed as clerks, construction workers, buyers, doctors, nurses, and even priests. Years after both she and Juan had died, long-forgotten warehouses were found containing masses of undistributed merchandise.

Perón made many appearances before her people, always dressed in sumptuous clothing and bedecked with fabulous jewels. She believed the people wanted to see her as a Cinderella, thinking that if Perón could rise to such heights, then perhaps they could as well. The people loved their Evita, or little Eva. And she loved being loved by them. She became their idol. They knew she shared their working-class background, and this further endeared her to them.

Eva Perón loved to distribute gifts to children. Here she appears at one of the many state functions set up for that purpose. (National Archives)

But Perón did more than run her foundation. She organized the first Argentinian women's party and pushed to get the vote for women so more people could vote for her husband. In 1951, as Juan prepared for his second term as president, Eva hoped to run as his vice president. At first Juan liked the idea, but his top military advisers made it clear that they would not support his candidacy if she ran. They didn't want a woman a heartbeat away from being commander in chief of the armed forces. Because Juan asked her to, Eva turned down the nomination.

Eva's health had always been fragile, and after Juan's second election, she became truly ill. For months she refused treatment and insisted on keeping up her grueling work schedule. Her doctors told her she needed a hysterectomy, but she thought they were conspiring against her. When it became apparent they had been telling the truth, it was too late. She died on July 26, 1952, from uterine cancer.

But her story didn't end with her death. Juan Perón refused to bury her. Instead, he had her body embalmed and placed in a glass coffin that remained on display so that the people could come to see her. Her corpse remained intact longer than Juan's presidency.

He remained in power for three years after Eva's death, but his downfall had begun long before. Between the constant salary raises, increased worker benefits, Eva's foundation, and their own lavish lifestyle, the Peróns had bankrupted Argentina. In 1955, Perón was forced out of office. He fled to Spain.

The people of Argentina were angry with Juan Perón, but their love of Eva remained constant. The people who had ousted Juan wanted to erase Eva's memory from the minds of the people. They were afraid that if her body remained in Argentina, it would become a symbol around which to organize a protest movement. To prevent this, her body was stolen and shipped to a secret hiding place in Italy.

In 1971, Eva's body was suddenly found and returned to Juan Perón, who was living with his new wife in Madrid. In 1973, another revolution had occurred in Argentina and Juan was called back from Spain to take his place once again as president. His new wife, Isabella, achieved what Eva had not. She became Juan's vice president and, when he died less than a year after taking office, Isabella succeeded him as president. She was not effective and her term lasted only a few months, but she did have Eva's corpse flown home and buried in a state ceremony.

"Without fanaticism one cannot accomplish anything."

—Eva Perón

Eva Perón was so beloved by some of Argentina's people that after she died, her name was proposed to the Pope as a candidate for sainthood. But not everyone loved her. Members of Argentina's wealthy classes said she was nothing more than an ambitious opportunist who exploited the people and bled Argentina's treasury. Her story inspired a long-running Broadway play, *Evita*, first produced in 1980, a movie by the same name made in 1996, and numerous books.

Chronology

May 7, 1919	Eva Marie Ibaguren born in Los Toldos, Argentina
1926	Eva's father, Juan Duarte, dies
1934	Eva Duarte goes to Buenos Aires to pursue acting career
1941	stars in radio drama series
1943	meets Colonel Juan Perón
October 21, 1945	Eva and Juan Perón marry
1946	Juan Perón elected president
1947	Eva Perón travels to Spain, France, and Italy
1948	opens Eva Perón Foundation
1949	forms Peronista Feminist Party
July 26, 1952	Eva Perón dies
1955	Juan Perón forced out of Argentina; Eva's body stolen
1974	Eva's body returned to Argentina and buried

Further Reading

Ashby, Ruth and Deborah Gore Ohrn. Eds. *Herstory.* New York: Viking, 1995. Contains good short profile of Eva Perón.

Barnes, John. *Evita: First Lady.* New York: Grove Press, 1978. Thorough biography of Perón and her rise to power.

Eloy, Tomas Martinez. *Santa Evita.* New York: Knopf, 1996. Blend of fiction, essay, and memoir. Story is told from after her death, but gives excellent picture of her life.

Fraser, Nicholas and Marysa Navarro. *Eva Peron.* New York: W.W. Norton: 1980. A thorough biography that examines Eva's strange story.

Nagel, Rob and Anne Commire. "Juan Domingo Perón and Eva Marie Duarte de Perón." *World Leaders: People Who Shaped the World,* Gale Research: 1994. Gives balanced overview of both Eva and Juan Perón.

Ortiz, Alicia Dujuorne. *Eva Perón.* New York: St. Martin's Press: 1996. A new biography of Eva Perón drawing on material formerly unavailable.

Margaret Thatcher, prime minister of Britain from 1979 to 1990, was the first woman to head a major Western country. She was also the longest serving British prime minister in the 20th century. (Courtesy Margaret Thatcher)

Margaret Thatcher of Britain

(1925–)

Margaret Thatcher, prime minister of Britain, was in her room at the Grand Hotel in Brighton. She had spent hours going over her notes for the 1984 Conservative Party Conference due to begin the next morning. Wearily, she looked at the clock. It was 2:45 A.M. But before she could wash up and go to bed, there was one final set of papers to be checked. Just as she reached for them, she heard a loud blast and felt the room shake.

A bomb had exploded somewhere in the hotel. The ceiling and walls in Thatcher's bathroom collapsed—if she been in the bathroom washing up, she might well have been killed. Throughout the hotel, windows shattered and walls crumbled. Thatcher and several other guests were quickly evacuated. Not everyone had been so lucky. Five cabinet members were killed and two received injuries that left them permanently crippled. The bomb had been planted by Irish Republican Army terrorists as part of their ongoing war against the British government.

Thatcher's personal courage in the face of this tragedy showed her to be a true leader. In spite of the inner turmoil she must have felt and her grief at the loss of her friends, she insisted the conference continue as scheduled. That afternoon, at the opening ceremony, she gave one of the most rousing speeches of her career.

Margaret Thatcher was prime minister of Britain from 1979 to 1990. She was the first woman to head a major government in modern Europe, and the longest serving British prime minister in 150 years. Unlike some women political leaders who inherited their positions through a father or husband, Margaret Thatcher earned hers strictly on her own.

Margaret Hilda Roberts was born on October 13, 1925, in Grantham, a small town about 100 miles from London. Her parents, Alfred and Beatrice, raised Margaret and her older sister, Muriel, with strict rules and old-fashioned beliefs in frugality, prayer, and hard work. Alfred Roberts was a grocer and part-time lay Methodist minister. Their flat (apartment), upstairs from the grocery, was a simple one. Their bathroom was an outhouse in the yard, and they had to heat bathwater on the stove.

As a young girl, Margaret had little time for play. The Roberts children were seldom allowed to go to the movies, and the family did not own a radio until Margaret was 10. The girls were encouraged to read, but only educational books. No novels, comics, or popular magazines were allowed.

During the week Margaret went to school, did homework, and practiced piano. Saturdays she worked in the shop, measuring tea and packaging biscuits. Sunday was church day. The entire family attended three services at the Methodist church where her father preached.

Aside from running his grocery and preaching, Alfred Roberts was active in local politics. From around the age of 10, Margaret accompanied her father to political meetings, helping him campaign when he ran for mayor and other positions. He also brought her with him to university extension courses, where he encouraged her to participate in discussions and ask questions.

As a young girl, Margaret kept to herself and had few close friends. Her father once told her never to follow the crowd, but to lead it. This is a lesson Margaret never forgot. She enjoyed competition, but only when she felt sure she would win. She did well on the debate team and was captain of the hockey team. When she won a prize for her piano playing and for a speech she gave, her teacher told her she was lucky. "No!" she said, "I earned those prizes."

Margaret's father may have been frugal, but he wanted Margaret to have the best education available and he sent her to private school. She did well in her studies, not because she was brilliant, but because she worked hard. Margaret wanted to go to Oxford, but there was a problem. Students entering Oxford were required to have studied Greek and Latin, subjects not offered by Margaret's small school, so her father hired private tutors to teach her those subjects. He also enrolled her in speech lessons to help her shed her middle-class accent so she would fit in better at Oxford among upper-class students.

At Oxford, Margaret enjoyed dancing, parties, and social drinking—activities strictly frowned on by her father. She applied to the debating society, but at that time no women were allowed. Instead, she joined the student political Conservative Club and she soon became the club's first female president.

From the time she had accompanied her father to his meetings in Grantham, Margaret knew she wanted to be a politician. But most politicians did not earn enough money to live on, so Margaret majored in chemistry instead of political science. She did not give up on her goal though. Shortly before she graduated, she

"No great goal was ever easily achieved."

—Margaret Thatcher

told an acquaintance, "I am going to be a member of Parliament." For a girl, especially a girl from a middle-class background with no connections, this was a high ambition.

After graduation, Margaret went to work as a research chemist. She also began preparing herself for her future political career by running as the Conservative representative to Parliament for the small town of Dartford. Since Dartford nearly always voted the Labour ticket, she stood little chance of winning, but she knew the experience of campaigning would be invaluable.

Margaret met Denis Thatcher, a wealthy businessman, at a Conservative Party meeting. What began as a friendship ripened slowly into love despite the fact that Denis was divorced and far older than Margaret. Although neither set of parents approved of the match, Margaret and Denis married in 1951. With Denis's encouragement, Margaret quit her job and returned to school to study law to help her political career.

Two years after her marriage, Thatcher passed the bar exam and began her practice as a tax lawyer. That same year she gave birth to twins, Carol and Mark. Thatcher always tried to plan her life in the most pragmatic fashion. Although she hadn't planned on twins, this too turned out to be practical. She had wanted two children and now had them without having to go through another pregnancy.

For the next several years, she managed to care for her children, run her law practice, and pursue her political career. In 1959, after three unsuccessful tries, she finally was elected as a Member of Parliament representing the Conservative Party for Finchley, a suburb of London.

For the next 11 years, she worked hard and was rewarded with increasingly important appointments. In 1970, she was named minister of education, a major post. For years, the government had provided free milk to all children in school. One of Thatcher's first acts was to cut government spending

The British prime minister lives and works in this very plain dwelling at 10 Downing Street. Other than the guards posted outside the door, it looks no different from all the other townhouses on the same block. (Courtesy British Tourist Authority)

by limiting the free milk to children under seven years old. Thousands of parents protested this move, chanting "Thatcher, Thatcher milk snatcher!" But she held firm and refused to back down.

In Britain the position of prime minister is not directly elected by the people. The people vote for a party to be the majority party and lead Parliament. Whoever is the leader of the winning party usually, but not always, becomes prime minister. The leading party is called the majority and the opposition is called the minority. In 1975, the Conservatives, who had held the majority, lost the election. At that time, Thatcher was chosen as leader of the Conservative Party. For four years, the Conservatives were the minority party, but in 1979, they won another election and Margaret Thatcher took her place as Britain's first woman prime minister.

In the years since the end of World War II, Britain had become increasingly socialist. Socialism is a system of economics under which the government owns major industries such as airlines, railroads, and oil production. Under socialism, the government is also responsible for medical care and insurance. Thatcher felt that many of the government-run programs were draining the economy and taking initiative away from individuals. She wanted to sell government-owned industries to private investors, to encourage people to purchase their own homes, and to cut welfare and social service payments. In one of her campaign speeches, she said, "Unless we change our ways and our direction, our greatness as a nation will soon be a footnote in the history books, a distant memory of an offshore island, lost in the mists of time like Camelot, remembered kindly for its noble past."

She knew her programs would hurt many people, but she felt she was helping to foster greater personal responsibility, which in turn would help restore the sense of British pride and self-reliance she felt had been lost. Though many people supported her programs, others felt they were too harsh.

But when Britain's economy began to improve, she gained the respect of both her fellow politicians and many of the British people. Thatcher may have been highly respected, but she was not particularly well liked. She had a fierce temper and would often scream at those who did not agree with her. She chose for her Cabinet members only those who would support her and fired or demoted those who did not. She was criticized for this, but it is a move practically every politician the world over makes. She was also criticized for her lack of support for women's causes.

As often happens in politics, events come along that can make or break a leader. This happened in 1982 when Argentina claimed ownership of the Falklands, a tiny chain of islands off the coast of Argentina in South America. The islands had been part of the British Commonwealth for more than 150 years and most of the inhabitants considered themselves British. Thatcher vowed to protect the Falklands, even if it meant going to war. She followed through with her threat to send British ships and planes across the ocean to fight. The people of Britain stood proudly behind Thatcher's decision.

"If you have a sense of purpose and a sense of direction, I believe people will follow you. Democracy isn't just about deducing what the people want. Democracy is leading the people as well."

—Margaret Thatcher

One of the very few times Thatcher showed any emotion in public was when she received word of British deaths and casualties in this short war.

The victory in the Falklands helped Thatcher win her second term as prime minister. As part of her move to strengthen individual responsibility and lessen government control over business, she waged a long and bitter battle with the labor unions. Her persistence paid off. The unions lost their stronghold over Britain's coal mines and other essential industries.

Her nickname, the Iron Lady, was given to her by the Soviet Union because of her uncompromisingly hard stand against communism. Though the name was not meant as a compliment, Thatcher turned it into one. She liked the image of being an "iron lady." But she did not like some of the other nicknames she was given, such as Attilla the Hen, or simply, "That Woman," by people who felt her programs were too harsh.

Despite her detractors, she gained enough support to win a third term as prime minister. Unlike in the United States, where once a president is elected, he always remains in office for his full term, in England, a vote of confidence can be called for any time a majority of the members of Parliament feel it is necessary. If the prime minister does not receive a majority of votes supporting him or her, the minister must step down. When Thatcher proposed a new poll tax in 1990, several members of Parliament who opposed the new tax called for a vote of confidence. Thatcher lost her position as party leader and as prime minister.

Thatcher was then 65, but she was not ready to retire. Instead, she said she was beginning a new phase of her life. She retained her seat in Parliament as representative for Finchley, set up the Thatcher Foundation to help develop private investment in eastern Europe, and began writing her memoirs. She also traveled around the world speaking on international and business issues.

In 1992, Thatcher was given one of England's highest honors. She was made baroness Thatcher of Kesteven. As a member of the peerage, Thatcher gave up her position as a member of the House of Commons to take a lifetime seat in the House of Lords. Her memoirs were published in two volumes, one in 1993 and the other in 1995.

Her legacy to the British people will be debated for many years to come. She certainly helped to restore British pride. She reorganized the economic system. But although much of England's economy has improved as a result of her programs, she was not able to keep inflation down, nor was she able to reduce the high unemployment from which much of England still suffers. Yet, in spite of this, Margaret Thatcher will long be remembered as one of England's strongest prime ministers.

Chronology

October 13, 1925	Margaret Hilda Roberts born in Grantham, England
1943	enters Somerville College at Oxford

1947	graduates from Oxford University with a degree in chemistry
1949	runs as member of Parliament for Dartford
1951	marries Denis Thatcher
1953	gives birth to twins, Mark and Carol
1953	Thatcher begins her law practice
1959	elected as member of Parliament for Finchley
1970	appointed minister of education
1975	elected leader of Conservative Party
1979	elected prime minister
1982	Falkland Islands War
1983	Thatcher's second term as prime minister
October 11, 1984	IRA bombs Brighton hotel
1987	Thatcher's third term as prime minister
1990	steps down as prime minister
1992	elevated to the peerage as baroness Thatcher of Kesteven

Further Reading

Faber, Doris. *Margaret Thatcher: Britain's Iron Lady*. New York: Viking Kestrel, 1985. A highly readable young adult biography.

Hughes, Libby. *Madam Prime Minister: A Biography of Margaret Thatcher*. Minneapolis: Dillon Press, 1989. Written for young adults, this book examines life of Thatcher and her rise to power. Includes glimpses of her personal life.

Moskin, Marietta D. *Margaret Thatcher of Great Britain*. Englewood Cliffs, New Jersey: Julian Messner, 1990. A young adult biography that chronicles Thatcher's rise to power.

Thatcher, Margaret. *The Downing Street Years*. New York: HarperCollins, 1993. Volume one of her memoirs.

———. *The Path to Power*. New York: HarperCollins, 1995. Volume two of her memoirs.

Violeta Chamorro, who helped to rid Nicaragua of two repressive regimes, served as her country's first democratically elected president from 1990 to 1996. (Courtesy D.I.P.P. Embassy of Nicaragua)

Violeta Chamorro of Nicaragua

(1929–   )

On the morning of June 26, 1986, when Violeta Barrios Chamorro, owner and publisher of *La Prensa*, Nicaragua's leading newspaper, arrived at her office, she was greeted by armed government soldiers blocking the entrance. They ushered her into her office and ordered her to shut down her presses and fire her reporters. The soldiers waited until everyone had left, then nailed boards across the front door. Chamorro wasn't really surprised at this action, because for the past several months she had been running articles criticizing the Sandinista government's increasingly repressive rule. She may even have smiled at the irony of the situation.

Seven years earlier, Chamorro's paper had supported the Sandinistas, who were leading a revolution to overthrow the Somoza government, a dictatorship that had ruled Nicaragua for many years. The revolution was successful, and after the Sandinistas took over, Chamorro was invited to became part of a special committee, called a junta, that would run the country until a democratic government could be established.

But it didn't take Chamorro long to realize that the Sandinistas were committed to establishing a communist government in Nicaragua, not a democratic one. She left the junta and once again used her newspaper to criticize the government—this time the Sandinistas. Revolution in Nicaragua continued.

Finally, after 10 years, the Sandinistas agreed to a free election. Daniel Ortega ran for the Sandinista party, and Violeta Chamorro ran as the leader of the National Opposition Union Party. The people chose Violeta Chamorro as their new president. When she stood on the dais of the Estadio Nacional (National Stadium) to take her oath of office, she was greeted by thunderous applause from her supporters—and by a barrage of plastic bags filled with soda pop from supporters of the Sandinista party. And while soda pop as a weapon was far preferable to bullets, the demonstration was just one indication of the widespread disagreement still tearing Nicaragua apart.

Violeta Barrios was born in Rivas, Nicaragua, on October 18, 1929. The Barrios family, which included eight children, owned several farms and cattle ranches and were among Nicaragua's wealthiest and most influential. Violeta's early childhood revolved around her family, school, and church. When she was 15, she was sent to a private Catholic school in San Antonio, Texas. After graduating from high school, she attended Blackstone College in Virginia, but dropped out at the end of her first year because her father died and she wanted to return to her family in Nicaragua.

The following year one of her brothers introduced her to Pedro Joaquin Chamorro. Violeta and Pedro were married in 1950, and Violeta fully expected her life to follow the traditional pattern for wealthy upper-class Nicaraguans. But her life turned out to be far from traditional.

Pedro, a journalist whose family owned *La Prensa*, wrote articles criticizing the dictatorship of the Somoza family, who had ruled the country since the 1930s. Because of this he was repeatedly jailed and harassed by the Somoza government. In 1957, he was forced to close his newspaper and the family was banished to a remote town near Costa Rica. He and Violeta fled across the border, where they joined a guerrilla group preparing to overthrow the Somozas. This was a difficult time for Violeta. She missed her children, whom she had to leave behind, and during her exile she conceived a fifth child, who died at birth.

In 1959, the Chamorros were allowed to return to Nicaragua and to reopen *La Prensa*. Though he knew it was dangerous, Pedro once again wrote articles criticizing the Somozas. As before, he was repeatedly harassed and jailed. Violeta visited Pedro in jail, bringing him news of the children and offering him her moral support. She later said it was her faith in God and her religion that sustained her through those difficult years.

One day Violeta's worst fears were realized. Pedro was gunned down by assassins on January 10, 1978. Though it was never proven, Violeta was sure his murderers had been sent by Somoza. Pedro was proclaimed one of Nicaragua's greatest heroes. Hundreds of thousands of Nicaraguans mourned him.

For 18 months following his death, there were riots and demonstrations against the Somoza regime. Many of these demonstrations were led by the Sandinista National Liberation Front, a guerrilla army that had formed in the early 1960s to overthrow the Somoza government. Somoza supporters countered with their own riots and demonstrations. Chamorro backed the Sandinistas. She published articles supporting their cause in *La Prensa,* and when friends of Pedro's sent her a gift of $100,000, she donated half of it to the Sandinistas.

Chamorro hoped the Sandinistas would help bring democracy to Nicaragua, but others were afraid the Sandinistas would only replace one dictatorship with another. Just as the Sandinistas had formed to support opposition to the Somozas, another group now formed to oppose the Sandinistas. The new opposition called themselves the Contras. Throughout the country, loyalties were divided among the Somoza supporters, the Sandinistas, and the Contras. These differences were reflected in Chamorro's own family. Two of her children were strong Sandinista supporters, one was virulently anti-Sandinista, and one, like Chamorro herself, hoped the Sandinistas and the Contras could find a way to work together. But Chamorro refused to allow politics to interfere with family relationships. She declared her home a politics-free zone, and each Sunday the entire family gathered for dinner—where no political discussion was allowed.

The Sandinistas received much of their support from the Soviet Union and Cuba, both communist countries. The United States supported Somoza because he was against communism. But as the extent of Somoza's corruption and repression was made more public, U.S. support was withdrawn. In 1979, the Sandinistas—led by Daniel Ortega—finally brought down Somoza's government. Somoza fled Nicaragua and was later assassinated in Paraguay.

At first, after withdrawing its support of Somoza, the United States openly backed the Contras. Then, when the U.S. Congress refused to allocate more funds for this support, the CIA took over. Operating in secret, they supplied guns and training to the Contras, helping them grow into a well-armed fighting force.

In the late 1980s, the communist governments in the Soviet Union and other European countries were collapsing and could no longer offer support to the Sandinistas in Nicaragua. This situation forced the Sandinistas to back down. Former United States president Jimmy Carter and a panel of United Nations supporters were called in to monitor Nicaragua's first free election in its 170-year existence as an independent country. Daniel Ortega ran on the Sandinista ticket. Chamorro was asked to head the opposition, a coalition of fourteen other parties. At first Chamorro was reluctant to run. But because she had pledged herself to fulfilling Pedro's dream of freedom for Nicaragua, she accepted.

Most of the world thought Ortega would win. He was an experienced politician who knew how to run a slick professional campaign. Chamorro, who had broken her leg a few months earlier, campaigned from a wheelchair. Instead of making fancy speeches, she simply spoke from her heart, promising to do her best to bring peace to her wartorn country, to end compulsory military service, to free all political prisoners, and to run a democratic government.

On February 25, 1990, Violeta Chamorro was elected president. She had a tremendous job facing her. Her country was in almost total ruin. Though a truce had been called, all fighting had not stopped. Before many Contras agreed to turn in their guns, they wanted assurances of jobs and land. These demands were not easy to meet. Most private land and

"There cannot be sovereignty without peace; no sovereignty without liberty. But to have liberty you must respect the rule of the law, other people's morals and opinions, and private property as well."

—Violeta Chamorro

nearly all industry had been nationalized by the Sandinistas. Figuring out a fair way to return the land and business to private ownership was a formidable task.

Everyone, including members of her own party, tried to tell Chamorro what to do. She listened to advice but made her own decisions. She once told a *New York Times* reporter, "I have enormous faith in God. He will illuminate and show me how to do what my conscience dictates."

She was determined that if nothing else, she would end the violence and bloodshed that had wracked her country for so long. And as she had done with her own family, she tried to bring opposing sides together to work out their differences over a table instead of with guns. She asked the Sandinistas to work with her to rebuild the country. In the spirit of

Violeta Chamorro folds the presidential sash and hands it to Ivan Escobar, president of the National Assembly, marking the end of her six-year term as president of Nicaragua, January 10, 1997. This date was the ninth anniversary of the assassination of Chamorro's husband, Pedro Joaquin Chamorro. (AP/Wide World Photos)

reconciliation and cooperation, she offered Daniel Ortega a seat in her government and allowed Humberto Ortega, his brother, to continue as leader of the army. Many people criticized these appointments because they thought the Sandinistas would overpower Chamorro and resume their leadership of the government.

"Reconciliation is more beautiful than victory."

—Violeta Chamorro

Their fears did not come true. Chamorro convinced most of the Contras to turn in their guns. She fulfilled her promise to release political prisoners. She drastically reduced the size of the army and ended compulsory military service.

There was much she could not accomplish. During the first four years of her presidency, there was little growth in the economy and little progress in returning land and industry to private ownership. Millions of people suffered from disease and extreme poverty. There was a lack of schools and hospitals. In addition, Nicaragua was devastated by a major earthquake, a volcanic eruption, and massive flooding. In spite of these calamities, some progress had been made by the end of her six-year term of office. Farms were producing profitable crops. Foreign investment was helping expand the economy. New schools and hospitals had been built.

But most of all, Chamorro had done what no one else in the history of Nicaragua had. When she was elected she said, "My dream is that if we accomplish the reforms I would propose, my presidential sash will one day be passed to a duly elected democratic successor." When her term of office ended in October 1996, she was succeeded by Arnoldo Alemán in the country's second consecutive democratically held election. She might not have accomplished all the reforms she had hoped for, but she did establish a precedent of democracy. For that she will be remembered and revered in Nicaragua's history.

Violeta Chamorro has returned to private life, and Arnold Alemán has the task of maintaining the democratic government Chamorro established. Whether or not this will happen remains to be seen. Nicaragua still has many problems to solve. There are widespread economic problems and poverty, especialy among Nicaraguans of Indian descent. There are bands of criminals roaming the countryside attacking tourists. And perhaps most of all, leaders of both the Old Samoza and Sandinista parties are still very much active in Nicaraguan politics. If the new president, Arnoldo Alemán, cannot solve his country's problems, the country may well revert to a dictatorship in the future.

Chronology

October 18, 1929	Violeta Barrios born in Rivas, Nicaragua
1950	marries Pedro Joaquin Chamorro, publisher of *La Prensa*
1962	Sandinista movement begins
January 10, 1978	Pedro Chamorro assassinated
1979	Violeta Chamorro takes over paper, continues opposition to Somoza government
1979	Somoza flees country
1979	Chamorro joins Sandinista junta
1980	resigns junta, resumes publication of paper
1986	Sandinista government shuts down *La Prensa*

February 25, 1990   Chamorro is elected president in Nicara-
                     gua's first free election
1996   succeeded by Arnoldo Alemán

Further Reading

Ashby, Ruth and Deborah Gore Ohrn. Eds. *Herstory*. New York: Viking, 1995. Contains a brief profile of Chamorro.

Chamorro, Violeta Barrios de. *Dreams of the Heart*. New York: Simon & Schuster, 1996. Chamorro's autobiography and memoirs.

Liswood, Laura A. *Women World Leaders: Fifteen Great Politicians Tell Their Stories*. New York: HarperCollins, 1995. Contains profiles of Chamorro as well as others in this book.

President of the Republic of the Philippines from 1986 to 1992, Corazon Aquino restored democracy to her country after helping to oust dictator Ferdinand Marcos. (Courtesy Corazon Aquino)

Corazon Aquino of the Philippines

(1933–)

C ory! Cory! Cory! Throughout the Philippine Islands, millions cheered their new president, Corazon Aquino. Most of the world was stunned at Aquino's victory. Cory Aquino had never intended to run for president. She was not a politician.

Corazon Aquino's path from quiet housewife to president of the Philippines began on the day her husband, Benigno, was shot through the head as he stepped off the plane that brought him back to Manila from the family's temporary home in the United States.

Cory had returned to the Philippines not to run for office but to arrange her husband's funeral. Instead, she assumed leadership and led her followers in a revolution of people power that successfully overthrew Ferdinand Marcos, the dictator who had ordered the murder of her husband and who had held the Philippines in his grip for more than 20 years.

Maria Corazon Cojuangco was born on January 25, 1933, in Tarlac, a small province about 50 miles north of Manila. She was the sixth of eight children. At that time, the Philippines was a territory of the United States, but in 1946, the chain of islands became an independent nation. The Cojuangcos were among the islands' wealthiest and most influential families. Besides owning a large sugar plantation, both Cory's grandfather and father had been congressmen.

When Cory was 13, her family sent her to the United States to attend a Catholic high school. Later, she attended a Catholic college, Mount Saint Vincent, in New York, where she earned a B.A. in French and math. Throughout her schooling, her classmates and teachers recall her as very shy and quite serious.

After college, she returned to the Philippines and enrolled in law school but dropped out after one semester to marry Benigno "Ninoy" Aquino, whom she had met the previous year during a school vacation. Ninoy was a journalist and popular young politician. For 20 years, Cory devoted her life to raising their five children and fulfilling her role as a dutiful wife while Ninoy established himself as a popular politician. By 1965, he had held positions as mayor, governor, and senator. He was also the leader of those opposing President Ferdinand Marcos's increasingly corrupt administration.

In 1972, instead of stepping down at the end of his term as president as called for in the constitution, Marcos declared martial law (rule under the military), took over the government, and declared himself dictator. Ninoy and others who opposed Marcos were arrested and sent to prison.

Ninoy's arrest was the beginning of a new life for Cory—a life of hardship she had never imagined. At first, nobody would tell her where Ninoy had been taken or whether he was alive or dead. But Aquino was determined to find out. Carrying her youngest child with her, she trekked from island to island, going from prison to prison looking for him. Often, she was forced to wait for hours in drenching rain or unrelenting tropical sun outside the prison gates before anyone would even speak with her. Finally, after 43 days, she found him. When she saw him she was shocked at how weak and disheartened he was. He told her he had been kept in solitary confinement and had been tortured.

The prison officials told Aquino she could visit, but only infrequently. That wasn't good enough for her. She pestered the officials until she was granted permission to visit every week. Then, each week, she was subjected to humiliating body searches and scathing insults from the guards. For anyone, but especially for a person as modest and as shy as Aquino, this was a terrible ordeal.

After two years, Cory convinced the authorities to grant her permission for an overnight visit. When she was admitted to Ninoy's cell, the first thing she did was to take a towel from her suitcase and cover the two-way mirror through which the prison guards always watched her husband. On Christmas and Easter, she brought the children, and the entire family slept on blankets on the floor of the cell.

Aquino did much more than merely visit her husband. She helped to keep the opposition movement alive by carrying messages from Ninoy to the press and to his supporters. When Ninoy declared a hunger strike Cory smuggled vitamin pills to him and later held press conferences to bring his message of freedom to the people. Speaking to large crowds was a painful ordeal for Cory. She once told a reporter that before she could muster the courage to speak for the first time, she had to calm herself by taking a tranquilizer.

In 1980, after several years' imprisonment, Ninoy suffered a serious heart attack. Cory was allowed to fly him to the United States for bypass surgery. Rather than return to prison, the Aquinos remained in the United States. Ninoy took a position as professor at Harvard University and secretly worked towards the day when he could rid his country of Marcos. Cory has often said these years were

"So long as I believe I have to do certain things, I will just go right ahead. That's how I run my life."

—Corazon Aquino

the happiest of her life. She was able to drop her role as political stand-in for Ninoy, which she found uncomfortable, and return to her preferred role as housewife and mother. She enjoyed cooking, watching television game shows, and helping her children with their homework.

In 1983, when Marcos said he would hold an open election, Ninoy decided to fly home to run against him. Cory was nervous. She knew this was a dangerous move, but as always, she supported her husband in his decision. She began packing her things, planning to join him in a few weeks. When she received the phone call telling her that her husband had been killed, she was devastated—but, as always in times of personal trouble, she drew on her deep religious faith for the strength to carry on.

When she arrived in Manila, she was surprised at her reception. Thousands of Ninoy's supporters greeted her at the airport. Most of them carried bright yellow banners, and as they made their way from the airport to the city, Aquino saw thousands of yellow ribbons and streamers hanging from trees. Later that day, Aquino donned a yellow dress and led two million mourners in a ten-hour funeral procession and vowed to carry on her husband's fight for freedom. Yellow had become the symbol of the anti-Marcos Freedom Party.

At first the Freedom Party urged voters not to vote in the upcoming election because they knew that Marcos had it rigged. But Aquino disagreed with this tactic. She thought people should vote to show Marcos they were tired of his corrupt rule. Marcos won the election, but because of Aquino's leadership, her party won more than 25 percent of the legislative assembly's seats.

In 1986, Marcos called for another election, hoping once and for all to defeat his opposition. The Freedom Party asked Corazon Aquino to run against him. At first, Aquino did not want to run. "Gosh, what do I know about being president?" she asked.

She reconsidered when the Marcos's corrupt courts found her husband's murderers not guilty. As always, she turned to her religion for strength and guidance. She said she hoped God would tell her she had no business running for president. But instead, she reported having a dream of being inside a church and seeing her husband's empty casket. She interpreted this to mean that his soul had been reborn in her and that it was her duty to run for president. With only six weeks to campaign, Aquino flew from one island to the next, appealing for support. She promised to restore democracy and freedom.

Aquino seemed to be a weak choice for president. Her inexperience showed when she responded to inquiries by saying, "Boy, you're asking me a hard question," instead of answering the question. However, she learned quickly and soon gained self-confidence. She told the people she offered them "hope for change," and her supporters formed the National Movement for Free Elections. The United States sent impartial observers to act as poll watchers. The elections were held and, although the government stole ballot boxes and threatened voters, Corazon Aquino won the popular vote.

But Marcos also declared himself the winner. A few days later, Aquino stood before the people and asked them to continue their nonviolent protests against Marcos. Marcos ordered tanks to plow through the protesters. The protesters stood firm and handed the soldiers flowers.

The soldiers refused to fire on their own people. Marcos's defense minister and his leading general defected to Aquino's

"Faith is not simply a patience which passively suffers until the storm is past. Rather, it is a spirit which bears things—with resignation, yes, but above all with blazing serene hope."

—Corazon Aquino

side. A few hours later, Marcos fled the country on a helicopter provided for his safe passage by the United States.

Corazon Aquino was president, but her struggles had barely begun. She was faced with problems that would have been staggering for a seasoned politician. For a woman with no prior leadership or political experience, the problems must have seemed overwhelming. Marcos had stolen millions of dollars from the country's treasury. The nation was overrun with debt. Thousands were unemployed. More than 70 percent of the people lived in terrible poverty. As if that was not enough, many opposing political factions were competing for power. They all thought Aquino was weak. Even her own party leaders thought she would be merely a figurehead while they made the important decisions. They were all wrong. Aquino was not weak at all. She listened to her advisers but made her own decisions. Not all of them were right, but they were her own and they were made in good faith.

She refused to move into the sumptuous Malacanang Palace, the traditional president's home. Instead, she lived and worked out of a modest guest house near the palace. One of her first official acts was to free 500 political prisoners. She tried to rid the army of Marcos supporters but was not fully successful in this. She called for a new constitution and wanted it in place within one year. She set strict guidelines for presidential powers, which included limiting any president to one term in office. She guaranteed her people that they would once again be entitled to the civil rights that had been taken away by Marcos, and she restored freedom of the press.

Aquino took her oath of office in February 1986. In July, a group still loyal to Marcos attempted a coup to overthrow her and reinstate their ousted leader. Marcos loyalists were not the only ones opposing Aquino. Seven times during her years in office, communists and several other political factions tried to wrest the government away from her.

Malacanang Palace, official residence and offices of the president (Courtesy Philippines Dept. of Tourism)

But Aquino persevered and held her country together. She remained in office for her full six-year term. While in office, she made a special effort to place qualified women in high government posts. She fulfilled her promise of remaining in office for only one term. When she stepped down, there was a free and fair election to choose her successor, Fidel Ramos. Aquino was happy with the choice. Ramos was the man she had endorsed. After the election, she told a reporter she felt relieved that she no longer had the burden of making decisions that would affect her entire country but only decisions about her own family.

Although some people criticized Aquino for being indecisive and for not accomplishing all of her goals, what she did accomplish is far more important that what she did not. Aside from dealing with political unrest and seven coup attempts during her term in office, the country was devastated by a major earthquake, a gigantic volcanic eruption, and massive flooding. Despite these problems, she did restore democracy. Her dedication and commitment to democracy paved the way for the renewed economic growth the country has enjoyed under President Ramos.

After her retirement as president, Aquino remained active in helping to improve conditions in her country. She chaired the Benigno S. Aquino, Jr., Foundation, which she established to assist in alleviating poverty, providing scholarships, and helping victims of natural disasters. She travels throughout the world as an ambassador of peace and has won several pretigious awards. She also now finds time to enjoy her five grandchildren.

Professor Belinda Aquino (no relation), Director of the Center for Philippine Studies at the University of Hawaii, says that Aquino's greatest legacy to her country was "providing a moral climate and moral leadership to put her country back on its feet after 14 years of dictatorship."

Chronology

January 25, 1933	Maria Corazon Cojuangco born in the Tarlac Province of the Philippines
1948	graduates Notre Dame Convent School in New York
1953	receives B.A. from College of Mount St. Vincent, New York
October 11, 1954	marries Benigno S. (Ninoy) Aquino, Jr.
1972	martial law declared and Benigno imprisoned
1978	Aquino speaks out for jailed husband
1980	Aquino and her family fly to U.S. due to husband's health
August 21, 1983	Ninoy Aquino assassinated at Manila Airport
1984	Corazon Aquino urges people to vote despite corruption of government

October 1986	Aquino asked to run for President
February 22, 1986	Marcos's defense minister and general defect to Aquino's side
February 25, 1986	Aquino and Ferdinand Marcos both claim victory; Marcos flees country
July 1986	first of seven coup attempts against Aquino government
February 2, 1987	voters approve new constitution
1990	major earthquake in Philippines
1991	eruption of Mount Pinatubo volcano
1992	Aquino succeeded by Fidel Ramos

Further Reading

Ashby, Ruth and Deborah Gore Ohrn. Eds. *Herstory*. New York: Viking, 1995. Contains a short, insightful profile.

Browne, Ray B. Ed. *Contemporary Heroes and Heroines*. Detroit: Gale Research, 1990. Contains a good chapter on Aquino.

Sheehy, Gail. "The Passage of Corazon Aquino." *Parade*, June 8, 1986. An excellent article on Aquino and her rise to power.

Newsweek, March 16, 1986. This entire issue is devoted to Aquino and the Philippines.

Scariano, Margaret M. *The Picture Life of Corazon Aquino*. Chicago: Franklin Watts, 1985. Traces Aquino's life, focusing on the challenges she faced after being elected.

Siegel, Beatrice. *Cory: Corazon Aquino and the Philippines*. New York: Lodestar Books, 1988. This biography focuses on the political background of the Philippines. Includes interview with Aquino.

Reid, Robert H. and Eileen Querro. *Corazon Aquino and the Brushfire Revolution*. Baton Rouge: Louisiana State University Press, 1995. Recommended by Professor Aquino of University of Hawaii.

For thirty years while Winnie Madikizela-Mandela's husband Nelson was in prison, she led protests demanding his freedom and the end of apartheid in South Africa. Nelson was freed in 1990. Apartheid ended in 1994; in the same year Nelson was elected president. Winnie Madikizela-Mandela is shown here addressing an audience at North-eastern University, Boston, Mass., April 19, 1996. (AP/Wide World Photos)

Winnie Madikizela-Mandela of South Africa

(1934–   )

For close to 30 years, the South African government tried to silence Winnie Madikizela-Mandela. They arrested her. They sent her to jail. They banned her. They even banished her to a remote village. But despite everything the government did, Winnie Madikizela-Mandela, known as *Umama Wethu*, the Mother of the Nation, led black South Africans in their long fight against Apartheid.

Then came headlines that shocked the world. Winnie Madikizela-Mandela was accused of participating in the brutal kidnapping and murder of 14-year-old Stompie Moeketsi. After a lengthy and widely publicized trial, she was found innocent of murder, but guilty of kidnapping and assault. She was given a six-year jail sentence, which was later suspended. Madikizela-Mandela claimed she was innocent of all charges. Many people thought this scandal would end Madikizela-Mandela's public life, but it was just one more tempest in the many storms she has lived through.

Winnie Nomzamo Madikizela was born on September 26, 1934, in Bizana, a rural village in South Africa. Her parents raised their nine children as devout Baptists but also instilled in them a strong sense of self-esteem and pride in their Xhosa tribal heritage. Winnie's father, Columbine Madikizela, the teacher at the village school, taught his students English, mathematics, science, and two very different versions of South Africa's history.

Most South Africans were blacks whose ancestors had lived in Africa for tens of thousands of years, but the country was run by the descendants of white Europeans who had established colonies in Africa in the 1600s. The government-supplied textbooks taught that white people had "civilized" Africa. The books claimed whites were superior to blacks and that they were the rightful owners and rulers of the land. But Winnie's father told a different story. He told of ancient civilizations and traditions of the Xhosas. He said that when white people came, they stole the Xhosas's land and their cattle and tried to enslave the people. Rather than submit to slavery, the Xhosas fled and set up villages far away from the white invaders. Years later, in her autobiography, Winnie said, "There is an anger that wakes up in you when you are a child and it builds up and determines the political consciousness of the black man."

When Winnie was 15, she left Bizana to attend high school in a larger village, then went on to Johannesburg, the capital, to study social work at the Jan Hofmeyer Social Centre. In Johannesburg, Winnie was introduced to the white world and to segregation. At school, she sat in on fiery meetings where students discussed ways in which they could protest the new laws established by the white government in 1948. These laws, known as apartheid, divided South Africans into four races: white, Bantu (black), Asian, and Colored—people of mixed race. Apartheid was designed to guarantee that whites, a minority of less than 30 percent of the population, maintained their position of power over all South Africans. Winnie listened, but at the time she was more interested in completing her studies than in protesting. In 1955, she obtained her degree and became a medical social worker.

In 1956, Winnie met Nelson Mandela, a lawyer and leader of the African National Congress (ANC), an organization protesting apartheid. Winnie was surprised at Nelson's interest in her. He was a famous person; he was 15 years older than she; and he was married. Yet the two were drawn to one another. Nelson's life became Winnie's. She joined the Women's League of the ANC, and in her spare time, counseled the families of those imprisoned by the government.

In 1958, Nelson divorced his first wife and married Winnie. It wasn't long before she was arrested and sent to jail for taking part in a demonstration. She was pregnant at the time and was afraid she would suffer a miscarriage because she was beaten so badly. Luckily, she did not. But she was fired from her job because her employer didn't want trouble with the authorities.

After three years of marriage, when Winnie was pregnant with her second child, the government outlawed the ANC and issued a warrant for Nelson's arrest. In order for him to continue his leadership, he went into hiding. For the next several years, Winnie had to raise her two daughters as a single parent, while at the same time letting them know they really did have a father. During these years, the only way Winnie could see her husband was through elaborate secret arrangements that put both of them at great risk.

Nelson was captured and arrested in 1962. Winnie was not arrested, but she was officially declared a "banned person." This meant she was not allowed to attend meetings, speak to the media, or write anything for publication. She had to obtain special permission to attend Nelson's trial.

When she showed up at court dressed in traditional tribal clothing, the authorities refused to admit her. From that day on, she wore European-style dresses but always chose green, gold, and black, the colors of the ANC. Nelson was first sentenced to several years of hard labor. The sentence was later changed to life imprisonment.

Winnie took Nelson's place as one of the leaders in the fight against apartheid. Defying her banning, she continued to participate in demonstrations and protests. Always, she spoke on her husband's behalf, calling for his freedom. From 1964 to 1985, the government imposed increasingly harsh measures against those who opposed apartheid.

Mandela lost several jobs because government officials threatened her employers if they kept her on. She was arrested several times on trumped-up charges. Once, she was kept in solitary confinement for nine months awaiting trial. She was tortured and never given enough to eat. Finally, when the trial was held, she was acquitted. But within days, she was rearrested and sent back to prison for another eight months. While in prison, she organized the other inmates and helped them demand more humane treatment. During this period, she sent her daughters to the neighboring country of Swaziland to attend school to protect them from government harassment.

After almost two years, Mandela was freed, but her banning orders were made even more restrictive than before. She was not allowed to have visitors in her own home or to leave her house except to go work. In 1976, the government blamed her for a series of violent demonstrations and riots. The police came to her home in the middle of the night.

> "It dawned on me that you either had to survive apartheid or you had to perish with it. I decided to survive."
>
> —Winnie Mandela

They threw stones on her roof and banged on her doors and windows. She was angry but not unduly alarmed, thinking she was being arrested yet again. She was dragged off to the police station and held overnight, but this time instead of being sent to jail, she was told she was being banished.

In the morning, police drove her to her house, where she found that everything she owned had been haphazardly tossed into a large truck. Mandela was told to get in the truck, where she sat amid her photographs, dishes, books, and clothing, which were all jumbled together. She was driven to the remote rural town of Brandfort to a house that had been empty for a long time and was so filled with dirt and trash that it took several hours of shoveling to clean it out. There were no toilet facilities, no running water, and no stove.

She was forbidden to leave Brandfort. She was forbidden to talk to more than one other person at a time. She was forbidden to communicate with journalists or to be quoted in any newspaper. Under constant police surveillance, she was ordered to report to the local police station once a week. She did, but she defiantly insisted on entering through the door marked WHITES ONLY. One time she was arrested for speaking to a neighbor—concerning the price of a chicken.

But even under these conditions, Madikizela-Mandela wasn't defeated. With the help of a few supporters, she opened a first-aid clinic, set up a nursery school, and started a soup kitchen. She organized women's and youth groups. Just as Winnie had vowed not to let the world forget about Nelson after he had been sent to prison, Winnie's supporters made sure the world did not forget Winnie when she was hidden away in Brandfort.

By the 1980s, countries around the world refused to do business with South African companies until the government ended apartheid. Even within South Africa, many whites called for the government to bring apartheid to an end. Violent demonstrations and protests erupted in several places. Thousands of people were killed.

In 1985, Mandela's home in Brandfort was firebombed and burned to the ground. Defying her banning orders, she fled to Soweto where, with the help of donations sent from people around the world, she built a large and luxurious new house. Her popularity among black South Africans soared. Once again, she was hailed as the Mother of the Nation and a leader of the freedom movement.

In 1986, the government lifted all restrictions against Winnie Madikizela-Mandela. For the first time in more than 20 years, she was free to speak to the world. When she spoke, the world heard not a woman calling for a peaceful solution but a woman calling for violence. "With our necklaces and matchsticks, we will liberate South Africa," she stated to a live TV audience. Necklacing was the horrific practice of throwing a tire filled with gasoline around a victim's neck and then throwing a match into the gasoline.

After this speech, she lost much of her support. She was criticized for advocating violence and refusing to work within the guidelines of the ANC. She, in turn, criticized the ANC for being too willing to compromise. Her reputation as a world hero was further tarnished when she was implicated in the 1988 Stompie Moeketsi murder case.

"I rediscovered the value of my soul in relation to my religious beliefs and most of all to the cause of my own people. . . . I had ideas and views of my own. I had my own commitment and I wasn't just a political ornament."

—Winnie Mandela

Winnie Madikizela-Mandela celebrates South Africa's new constitution, May 8, 1996. (AP/Wide World Photos)

But the fight against apartheid went on and was gradually being won. In 1990 the world cheered when Nelson Mandela was freed from prison. Within days of his release, he took his place as the leader of the ANC, which was once again recognized as a legal organization. Nelson was ready to work with the white government to bring a final end to apartheid. Winnie stood at her husband's side and rejoiced. Apartheid was over and a new era began for South Africa.

Both Winnie and Nelson Mandela had sacrificed many years of their lives to end apartheid. For 30 years, although they had been forced to live apart, they had presented a united front to the world. Unfortunately once Nelson was free, that united front crumbled when Nelson accused Winnie of having an affair with her lawyer.

In 1994 Nelson Mandela was chosen as president of South Africa in the country's first multiracial election. Winnie won a seat in the new parliament. In spite of their personal differences, Nelson appointed Winnie as deputy minister of arts, culture, science, and technology. However, after she publicly criticized him and his administration, he fired her from this position. In 1996, after a long and messy trial, Winnie and Nelson were divorced.

The last few years have been tumultuous for both the Mandelas and for South Africa. In spite of Winnie's tarnished reputation among whites and moderate blacks, she retained a loyal following among the more radical and younger blacks who felt changes were not being made quickly enough. Winnie openly criticized the ANC and lost her position as president of the Women's League but was reelected the following year.

Winnie Madikizela-Mandela continues to be a controversial figure. Whil she still has her supporters, many people see her as an advocate of violence instead of peace. Others think her position of power has corrupted her—she has been accused of several instances of financial misconduct, but none of the charges has been proven.

In December 1997, during hearings of a special Truth and Reconciliation Commission, which was set up to investigate atrocities that occured during the unrest of the 1980s, Madikizela-Mandela was once again accused of complicity in several assaults, kidnappings, and murders, including that of Stompie Moeketsi. Despite the many witnesses who testified against her, among whom were many important South African leaders, Madikizela-Mandela consistently denied all charges of personal involvement in any of the incidents cited. She did, however, say, "I am saying it is true, things went horribly wrong [in the 1980s]. I fully agree with that. And for that part of those painful years, when things went horribly wrong—and we were aware of the fact that there were factors that led to that—for that I am deeply sorry."

The comission had no powers of indictment, so no charges were filed, and all accusations remain allegations. But the hearings seem to have finally ended Madikezela-Mandela's political career—at least for the present.

At the time of the hearings, Madikizela-Mandela still held her seat as president of the ANC Women's League and hoped to be nominated for the position of deputy president of the ANC for the January 1998 elections. But she had been so discredited during the hearings that her nomination was withheld and she declared herself out of the running.

It may be true that Winnie Madikizela-Mandela was indeed guilty of the charges against her. But it is also true that she has long campaigned for better conditions for South Africa's poorest blacks, whose lives have changed little since the days of apartheid. It is also true that for close to 30 years, it was Winnie Madikizela-Mandela who was the symbol of freedom to millions of black South Africans, and her leadership that helped bring an end to apartheid.

Chronology

September 26, 1934	Winnie Madikizela born in Bizana, a district of Pondoland, South Africa
1952	graduates high school and goes to Johannesburg to attend college
1955	becomes medical social worker
1956	meets Nelson Mandela
1957	joins ANC Women's League
June 14, 1958	marries Nelson Mandela; jailed for protesting

1961	ANC is outlawed; Nelson Mandela goes into hiding
1962	Nelson Mandela is captured and arrested
1964	Nelson Mandela is sentenced to life in prison; Winnie is banned
1965	Mandela's banning made stricter
1969	jailed for 17 months
1976	new banning orders and banishment to Brandfort
1982	banning renewed for five more years
August 14, 1985	Winnie Mandela's house in Brandfort firebombed
1988	Mandela implicated in murder of Stompie Moeketsi
1990	Nelson Mandela freed from prison
1991	Winnie Mandela acquitted of murder but found guilty of complicity
1992	Winnie and Nelson Mandela are separated
1994	Nelson Mandela elected as president of South Africa; Winnie Mandela wins seat in Parliament; appointed as cabinet member; she is fired, rehired, then fired again.
1995	Winnie Mandela implicated in several scandals
1996	Winnie and Nelson Mandela divorced; Winnie Madikizela-Mandela retains her position as leader in ANC Women's League and holds seat in parliament
1997	Truth and Reconciliation Commision hearings lead to allegations of atrocities by Madikizela-Mandela; Madikizela-Mandela's nomination for deputy president of ANC is withdrawn

Further Reading

Brickhill, Joan. *South Africa: The End of Apartheid*. New York: Gloucester Press, 1991. Good background on South African history and apartheid to 1991.

Hoobler, Dorothy and Thomas Hoobler. *Mandela: The Man, The Struggle, The Triumph*. New York: Franklin Watts, 1991. Good background of South Africa for young adults. Also includes several segments on Winnie.

Mandela, Winnie. *Part of My Soul Went With Him*, Edited by Anne Benjamin. New York: Norton & Co., 1984. Collection of essays by Winnie about herself and her life.

Sithole, Nokwanda. "Winnie Mandela: Her Story." *Essence*, April 1994. Gives a good objective overview of her life to 1994.

Macdonald, Fiona. *Working for Equality*. New York: Hampstead Press, 1988. Excellent sections on Winnie Mandela, South Africa, and apartheid.

Texas congresswoman Barbara Jordan was the first African American and the first woman from a southern state to serve in Congress. Her decisive leadership paved the way for other African Americans to take their place in national politics. (Courtesy Barbara Jordan Archives, Texas Southern University, Houston, Texas)

Barbara Jordan of Texas
(1936–1996)

In 1973, a group of men working for President Richard Nixon, a Republican, broke into the Democratic Party's headquarters at the Watergate Hotel in Washington, D.C. The men were looking for any information that the Republican Party could use against the Democrats in next presidential election.

Nixon was accused of lying, of advising his top aides to commit perjury (lying under oath), and of tampering with evidence in an attempt to cover White House involvement in the break-in.

After a series of special investigations and hearings, the case was put before the House Judiciary Committee, which was charged with the awesome responsibility of deciding whether to send the president to trial—to impeach him.

Finally, after a year of deliberations and investigation, the committee was ready to vote. That day, millions of people across the nation sat transfixed in front of their television sets. Barbara Jordan, a recently elected congresswoman from Texas, was one of members of the committee. She had thought long and hard about her decision and what it would mean to the people of America. When it was her turn to speak, her rich, sonorous voice boomed out over the airways. "When the Constitution was completed on the Seventeenth of

September in 1787, I was not included in that 'We, the people,'" she said. She went on to point out that it was only "through the process of amendment, interpretation, and court decision . . ." that she (along with all other African Americans) was now included in "We the People." She spoke of her obligations concerning the question facing the committee on that day. She explained the seriousness of an impeachment charge. "It is to be used for high crimes and misdemeanors. For great misdemeanors," she said. "The President," she stated, "is sworn to uphold the Constitution and all the laws the Constitution protects." She went on to explain in clear and simple words exactly what Nixon's crimes against the constitution had been: his part in the coverup, his false statements, his advice to others to make false statements, and his attempts to interfere with the investigations.

"Today, I am an inquisitor," she said. "I shall not sit here and be an idle spectator to the diminution, the subversion, the destruction of the Constitution." Jordan then voted for impeachment. As soon as the proceedings were completed, she slipped into an empty room and broke into tears over the enormity of what she had done.

Before that day few people outside of Texas had heard of Barbara Jordan. But after that historic day, there were few who did not know her. After listening to her speak, one reporter wrote "If God is a woman, she must sound like that."

As it turned out, Richard Nixon resigned from his office. Impeachment proceedings were never actually carried out.

Barbara Charline Jordan was born on February 21, 1936, in Houston, Texas, the youngest of three daughters of Benjamin and Arlyne Patten Jordan. Her father was a clerk at a warehouse; he later became a Baptist minister. Her mother, often a featured speaker at her church, insisted not only that her children speak correct English but also that they clearly enunciate every syllable of every word.

Barbara's parents, both strict Baptists, frowned on dancing and movies as frivolous. But they did enjoy music, and each member of the family sang in the church choir and played an instrument. Barbara's was the guitar. The Jordans also instilled in their daughters the desire to strive always to be the best. Barbara loved and respected her parents, but thought they were too strict. The person who most influenced her life was her maternal grandfather, John Patten. He encouraged her to follow her own path instead of blindly following the rules of others.

Barbara grew up in the days when the South was still segregated, both by custom and law. She grew up in an all-black neighborhood and seldom risked leaving it for the foreign white world outside its boundaries. Her family was poor, but so were most of the people she knew, so she never felt disadvantaged.

Perhaps it was her mother's influence that made Jordan so adept at public speaking. She was a star member of her debating team at Phyllis Wheatley High School, where she won a trip to Chicago to compete in a nationwide contest that included both black and white students. Jordan won first prize.

Even as a young girl, Jordan's ambition was to do something that would really make a difference. She thought about becoming a pharmacist but rejected the idea because she felt her chances of making a real impact on the world would be limited. Then one day, Edith Sampson, an African-American lawyer, spoke to Jordan's high school class on Career Day. From that day on, Jordan knew she would become a lawyer.

After graduating from high school, she enrolled in Texas Southern University, an all-black college in Houston. She was the only female to join the debating club and was hurt and angry when the coach refused to allow her to travel with the team because he thought a young woman would be a distraction. Jordan kept asking. Her persistence paid off, and she traveled to contests throughout the country. In one contest, Jordan led her team to victory over the team from Harvard University. For a small African-American college to win over one of the most prestigious universities in the world was quite a triumph.

In her travels around the country, Jordan experienced both the full meaning of segregation in the South and the relative freedom of the North. In the South, the team had to carry its own food because restaurants wouldn't serve blacks. The team had to stay in out-of-the-way and rundown hotels. But in the North, they were welcomed in most restaurants and regular hotels. Jordan decided to complete her education in the North where she could enjoy greater freedom.

"We must exchange the philosophy of excuses—what I am is beyond my control—for the philosophy of responsibility."

—Barbara Jordan

After graduating from Texas Southern University *magna cum laude* (with highest honors), she was accepted into Boston University Law School. The class consisted of 592 white men and six women, only two of whom were African American. It didn't take Jordan long to discover that despite her high grades, she was far less well prepared than her classmates who had attended white colleges. She studied extra hard to make up her deficiencies and graduated with her law degree in 1959.

She returned to Houston and set up her law office in her parents' kitchen. Slowly, her practice and reputation grew. In 1960, she volunteered to campaign for John F. Kennedy, who was the Democratic presidential candidate. She began by making speeches to her local district but soon was the main speaker for all the black Democratic districts in Houston.

Jordan enjoyed practicing law but saw that the only way to really make an impact on society was to be part of the process of making laws, rather than representing clients accused of breaking them. She ran for the Texas House of Representatives in 1962, but lost. She tried in 1964 and lost again. But she didn't give up. In 1966, she became the first African American elected to the Texas senate since shortly after the Civil War and the first African-American woman ever elected to that office. Her victory was particularly noteworthy because she won the election opposing a white man.

At first, she was mistrusted by her white male colleagues, but it didn't take her long to gain their trust and respect. In 1968, she won another term. She pushed for laws that would protect ordinary working people, such as a minimum wage law that included household help and farm workers.

Jordan's next step was to make a bid for national office. She ran for and won a seat in the United States House of Representatives, which led to her seat on the House Judiciary Committee. However, before she left the Texas senate, eight senators who had greater seniority than she agreed to step aside so she could receive the very special honor of being named governor for a day. Jordan's father was among the many who took part in those gala ceremonies. Sadly, during the festivities, he suffered a stroke and died the next morning. But Jordan was grateful that he had the pleasure of sharing in her singular honor.

In Washington, her membership of the Judiciary Committee was only one part of her job. She worked consistently for

"I am neither a black politician nor a female politician, just a politician."

—Barbara Jordan

improved civil rights legislation, more support for education, and other laws to help working-class Americans.

In the early 1970s, Jordan, who was already afflicted with diabetes, high blood pressure, and several other health problems, learned she had multiple sclerosis, a degenerative disease of the central nervous system. She never spoke of her diseases and refused to allow them to interfere with her life, but as the multiple sclerosis worsened, she needed a walker to help support her weakened legs.

In 1976 Jordan was invited to be a keynote speaker at the Democratic National Convention. She was scheduled to speak on the final night. The scene was one of controlled chaos. Few people sat in their seats. Instead, they milled about the floor waving placards and banners. Human chains snaked up and down the aisles, shouting political slogans and chanting the names of favorite candidates. Practically no one paid attention to what was going on the stage at the front of the vast auditorium.

When it was Jordan's turn to speak, she walked to the podium, leaning on her walker. On stage, she let go of the walker and stood proud and tall. Within seconds, her powerful voice boomed out over the general melée on the floor. She opened her speech with these words: "One hundred and forty-four years ago, members of the Democratic Party met for the first time in convention to select their Presidential candidate. Since that time, Democrats have continued to convene once every four years to draft a party platform and nominate a Presidential candidate. Our meeting this week continues that tradition. There is something different and special about this opening night. I am a keynote speaker."

She went on to point out that never before had an African American been chosen to be a keynote speaker.

As she talked, people stopped shouting. They turned to the stage and stood quietly or took their seats. And they listened, spellbound, as Jordan spoke of the need for unity within the country and within the Democratic Party. She ended her speech by saying: "We are a people in a quandary about the present and in search of the future . . . We are a people in search of a national community." That speech is considered by many to be one of the most powerful speeches in the history of political conventions.

In 1979, after three terms in Congress, she left Washington and public life to accept a professorship at the Lyndon B. Johnson School of Public Affairs at the University of Texas at Austin. That same year, she also wrote her autobiography and hosted a radio program, "Crisis to Crisis with Jordan."

By that time her multiple sclerosis had worsened, confining her to a wheelchair. She also suffered from hypertension, diabetes, and leukemia. But, as she said in a 1992 interview, she felt she should "treat the limitations as irrelevant and refuse to let them be an impediment" to her life's work.

Jordan was as successful a teacher as she had been a politician and much loved by her students. She was awarded honorary degrees from Harvard, Princeton, and several other universities. For the first couple of years after her retirement from Washington, she was a sought-after speaker, but as the effects of her illness increased, she stayed closer to home, where she devoted her energies to her teaching career. In recognition of her many accomplishments and contributions to public service, she was accorded several special honors during her lifetime. In 1985 she was named Best Orator of the year by the Orators Hall of Fame. In 1990, she was inducted into the Women's Hall of Fame in Seneca Falls, New

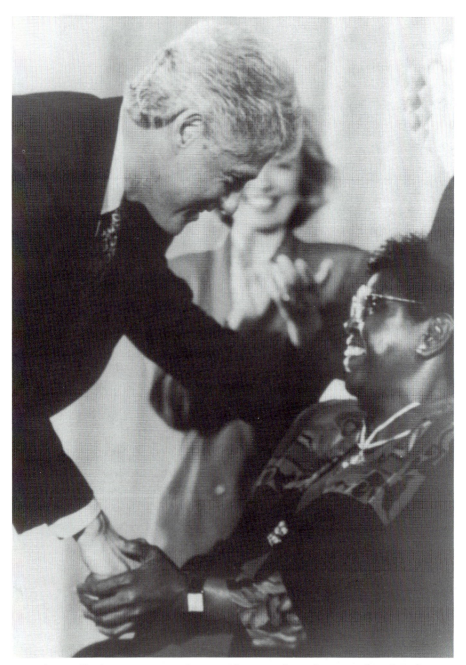

President Bill Clinton congratulates Barbara Jordan after awarding her the Presidential Medal of Honor. (Courtesy Barbara Jordan Archives, Texas Southern University, Houston, Texas)

York. In 1991, she was appointed as ethics adviser to Governor Ann Richards of Texas. In 1992, she was again the keynote speaker at the Democratic National Convention, where she once again was the only speaker to command the full attention of the audience. In 1994 she was awarded the Presidential Medal of Freedom, one of the highest tributes paid to a United States citizen.

Jordan was sometimes criticized for not being more militant regarding civil rights. However, she believed that cooperation was far more effective than disruptive or divisive behavior. Jordan worked toward greater understanding between all people.

When Jordan died of viral pneumonia, on January 17, 1996, the nation mourned her death. She was known for her passion for justice, her lifelong work to improve the lives of ordinary people, and her unstinting dedication and devotion to the Constitution and Declaration of Independence. Her funeral was attended by hundreds of admirers—public figures and private citizens, African Americans and whites. As a measure of the high regard in which she was held, President Bill Clinton attended her funeral. Her borrowed words Jordan herself had used during her 1976 keynote speech to pay her tribute. "Are we to be one people bound together by common spirit . . . or will we become a divided nation?"

Jordan kept her personal life intensely private. She never married. For many years she shared her home with her longtime companion Nancy Earl.

When Jordan was a youngster, she wanted more than anything else to do something remarkable with her life. Her ambitions were fulfilled to a greater degree than she would have thought possible. She will long be remembered as one of the country's outstanding women politicians as well as an outstanding educator.

Chronology

February 21, 1936	Barbara Jordan born in Houston, Texas
1952	graduates from Phyllis Wheatley High School; wins national oratorical contest
1956	graduates Texas Southern University
1959	graduates Boston University Law school
1962	runs for Texas House of Representatives; loses
1964	runs and loses again
1966	elected to Texas senate
1968	elected to second term in Texas senate
1972	honored as Texas governor for a day; elected to U.S. House of Representatives; serves on Judiciary Committee
1973	becomes ill with multiple sclerosis
1974	makes famous speech at House hearings regarding Richard Nixon's impeachment; wins second term in the House
1976	is keynote speaker at Democratic National Convention; wins her third congressional term
1979	retires from Congress, becomes professor at University of Texas
1982	appointed to Lyndon B. Johnson Centennial Chair of National Policy at University of Texas
1992	is keynote speaker for second time at Democratic National Convention
1994	is awarded Presidential Medal of Freedom
January 17, 1996	Barbara Jordan dies

Further Reading

Blue, Rose, and Corinne Naden. *Barbara Jordan*. New York: Chelsea House, 1992. A thorough young adult biography of Jordan's life through the early 1990s.

Jordan, Barbara and Shelby Hearon. *Barbara Jordan: A Self-Portrait*. Garden City, New York: Doubleday, 1979. Jordan's autobiography.

Patrick-Wexler, Diane. *Barbara Jordan*. Austin, Texas: Raintree-Steck Vaughn, 1996. A concise biography primarily for younger readers.

Gro Harlem Brundtland, *who served three terms as Norway's prime minister, proved her commitment to increasing the role of women in her country's government when she insisted that at least 40 percent of the candidates running for public office be women.* (Courtesy Gro Harlem Brundtland)

Gro Harlem Brundtland of Norway

(1 9 3 9 –   )

T he morning was clear, the water fairly calm. Prime Minister Gro (pronounced Grew) Harlem Brundtland and her husband, Arne, were enjoying the day sailing their 33-foot boat in one of Norway's many fjords (narrow ocean inlets). Suddenly the weather changed. Black storm clouds loomed overhead. Fierce winds beat the sails and whipped up the seas. The boat pitched about in the heavy waves. While Gro steered through the choppy waters, Arne worked furiously to take down the sails. But the wind and current were too fierce. Arne lost his footing and was washed overboard. The churning waters made it impossible for him to climb back into the boat. Gro grabbed a rope, threw it to her husband, wrapped the rope around his hands, and tied him to the stern of the boat. Then, she calmly maneuvered the boat through the storm, towing Arne back into safer waters and into port. During the three terms Brundtland served as prime minister of Norway, she showed the same quick thinking and decisive action.

Gro Harlem was born on April 20, 1939, in Oslo, Norway, at the start of World War II. By the time she was two years old, Norway had been occupied by Hitler's forces. Gro's parents, Gudmund and Inga Harlem, both of whom were active in the resistance movement, smuggled their daughter into Sweden, Norway's neutral neighbor, where she would be safe.

Gro returned to her family after the war. At the time, the prevailing attitude toward women in Norway was much like that in the rest of the world: girls were somehow less capable than boys in math and science; men made better leaders than women. But this was not the view in Gro's family. They instilled in her the firm belief that she could attain whatever goals she set for herself. She was close to both her parents but was particularly influenced by her father, who was personal physician to the prime minister. He was also active in the Labour Party and served as a member of the Labour cabinet for several years. Gro's interest in politics surfaced early. When she was seven years old, she joined the children's branch of the Labour Party, and later, in high school and university, she was active in student socialist unions.

After completing secondary school, she entered Oslo University to pursue premedical studies. While still a student, she met and fell in love with Arne Brundtland, who was studying international affairs. The young couple married and had their first child while they were still in school. Instead of socializing between classes, Brundtland found a quiet corner and nursed her baby.

In 1963, she obtained her medical degree and began practice as a pediatrician. In 1965, both she and Arne continued their studies in the United States, where Gro earned a master's degree in public health from Harvard University.

Back home in Norway, she put her public health degree to good use. Between 1966 and 1974, she held several national and municipal public health positions, beginning with her appointment as medical officer at the Norwegian Directorate of Health. That appointment led to her being named assistant medical director on Oslo's municipal health board. She also served as deputy director of the city's school health services and as a physician in the children's department at Rikshospital in Oslo.

She was, at the same time, becoming more active in her local Labour Party, where her outspoken advocacy for women's rights and more liberal abortion laws brought her to national attention.

As part of her studies in public health at Harvard University, Brundtland became involved in studying the effects of pollution on the environment. This interest resulted in her appointment in 1974 as minister of environmental affairs. As she became more actively involved in politics, her duties allowed her little time to tend house or care for her four children. Arne, a journalist who was able to do his work from a home office, took over running the household and caring for the children. This role reversal was not the only unusual thing about the Brundtland household. Arne thoroughly supported his wife's political career, but he didn't vote for her because while she was a member of the Labour party, he was a member of the Conservative party. Both Brundtlands have always claimed this difference made for interesting family discussions but presented no problems in their personal relationship.

During her tenure as minister of environmental affairs she promoted programs to establish nature preserves and campaigned for environmental protection and safer working conditions in Norway's newly discovered offshore oil reserves in the North Sea.

Brundtland did more than fulfill her duties as minister of the environment. From 1975 to 1981 she acted as deputy leader of the Norwegian Labour Party. In 1977 she was elected as Oslo's representative to the Storting (Norway's parliament), where she served on the finance and foreign affairs committees. In 1979 she was named deputy leader of her party, and in 1980 was named leader of the committee on foreign and constitutional affairs, a post she held until 1986 and again from 1989 to 1990.

In February 1981, the prime minister resigned, and Brundtland was named as his replacement, making her the country's first woman prime minister and, at 41, the youngest woman to head a modern government. Her first term as prime minister was a short one. In October 1981, the Labour party lost the election. Brundtland was still head of the party but no longer prime minister.

Because of her ongoing interest in the environment, in 1984 Brundtland joined the United Nations World Commission on Environment and Development, where she chaired worldwide hearings on environmental problems.

In 1986, the Labour Party won the election and, once again, Brundtland became prime minister. Brundtland, perhaps more than any other woman political leader, has actively promoted opportunities for the women of her country. One of her first actions as prime minister during her second term in office was to make a ruling that at least 40 percent of Labour Party candidates be women. She followed through with this by

Norway's seat of government, the Storting building, in Oslo, Norway
(Følgende kilde må oppgis ved bruk av bildet: Stortingsarkivet–Tiegens fotoatelier a.s. Parliament House Archives)

choosing women to fill eight of the 18 cabinet posts in her administration.

She won her third term as prime minister in 1990. During this campaign, a Conservative Party slogan read, "Do as Brundtland did. Choose a Conservative." She countered with a slogan of her own: "Do as Arne did. Choose Gro."

Her work as chairperson of the United Nations Environment Commission continued. In 1987, the commission issued their report, "Our Common Future," which became known as the Brundtland Report, urging governments and industry to assume more responsible positions in seeking solutions to such problems as the depletion of Earth's ozone layer by fluorocarbon chemicals in spray cans and the disposal of toxic and nuclear wastes. For several years, these proposals received little support, but after 173 nations held an environmental summit in 1993, many of her suggestions were implemented.

While she was touted internationally for her concern for the environment, at home she was criticized by some for not taking stronger measures to clean up Norway's polluted fjords and for her failure to take steps against Norway's whaling industry.

In 1992, Brundtland suffered a personal tragedy when one of her sons committed suicide. Soon after that incident, although she retained her position as prime minister, she gave up her position as party chairperson, saying she needed more time for her personal life.

Throughout her public career, Brundtland consistently urged the world's wealthier countries to work toward alleviating poverty in developing nations, not only through increased monetary help, but also through increased technological assistance and education. Under Brundtland's

"Women's roles and their chances in life to develop themselves are central to my thinking."

—Gro Harlem Brundtland

leadership, Norway committed one of the highest per capita foreign aid budgets in the world, an example she urged other countries to follow. The money thus raised, she felt, should be used for research into ways to decrease pollution and to develop technologies for energy conservation, cleaner fuels, and waste reduction. In an interview for *Technology Review* in 1993, she said, "Only by educating people and giving them a fair chance to break out of poverty can we help to find a sustainable relation between population and resources." In recognition of her many accomplishments in these areas, she was awarded the Third World Prize and the Indira Gandhi Prize in 1988, the Onassis Foundation's Delphi Prize in 1992, and the Charlemagne Prize in 1994.

In October 1996, Brundtland made a surprise announcement that she was resigning as prime minister. She said she would retain her position as Oslo's Storting representative and also planned to remain active in other ways. As of February 1998, she was being considered as the new head of the United Nations's World Health Organization. She would be the first woman to hold this position.

"The environment is where we all live; and development is what we all do in attempting to improve our lot within that abode. The two are inseparable."

—Gro Harlem Brundtland

Most Norwegians were sorry to lose Brundtland as their prime minister. They felt she had been a strong and capable leader who helped Norway to reach unprecedented economic stability and success. Almost universally loved and respected by her constituents, she was affectionately looked upon as "Mother Norway."

In her role as prime minister, she has been an important role model for young women the world over. She laughingly told of schoolchildren who sometimes asked her, "Can men be prime ministers, too?"

Chronology

April 20, 1939	Gro Harlem born in Oslo, Norway
1960	marries Arne Olav Brundtland
1963	Gro Harlem Brundtland receives M.D. degree from University of Oslo
1965	receives master of public health degree from Harvard University
1968–74	appointed assistant medical director on Oslo's municipal health board
1974	appointed minister of environmental affairs
1977	elected to Storting as representative from Oslo
February 3, 1981	appointed interim prime minister
April 1981	named Labour Party chairperson
October 14, 1981	Labour Party loses election; Gro Harlem Brundtland steps down as prime minister
1984	appointed chairperson of the United Nations World Commission on Environment and Development
1986	elected to second term as prime minister
1990	elected to third term as prime minister
1992	resigns post as party chairperson
October 1996	resigns post as prime minister

Further Reading

Brill, Alida. *A Rising Public Voice: Women in Politics Worldwide.* New York: Feminist Press, 1995. Contains a profile of Brundtland and others, along with an analysis of women politicians and the problems they face.

Kagda, Sakina, *Norway.* New York: Marshall Cavendish, 1995. Contains a profile of Brundtland. Also background material on the history, geography, culture, and lifestyles of Norway.

Principal chief Wilma Mankiller is shown here at Cherokee headquarters in Tahlequah, Oklahoma, October 1985. She was the first woman to head a major Native American tribe. (Courtesy Cherokee Nation, Sammy Still, photographer)

Wilma Mankiller of the Cherokee Nation

(1945–)

On November 20, 1969, a group of Native Americans took possession of Alcatraz, an abandoned prison on a tiny island in San Francisco Bay. They claimed the island was rightfully theirs because it had once belonged to their ancestors, and according to a long-forgotten treaty, any unused federal land must revert back to the Indians from whom it was taken.

The Native Americans involved in the Alcatraz takeover represented more than 20 tribes and came from all parts of the United States. Some came alone; others came with their entire families. They came to force the people of the United States to listen to their demands for more respect and recognition of their tribal heritages. They came to demand more and better opportunities for their peoples. They came to protest the U.S. government's long history of wrongs against Indians and the terrible conditions on reservations.

This was not an overnight television event. The protest lasted 18 months, during which hundreds of people camped out on the island. But those living on the island were only part of this protest. Those who chose to remain on the island could not have done so without the help of others who raised money for needed food and supplies and who ferried these supplies to the island.

Wilma Mankiller Olaya, who had been born on Cherokee tribal lands in Oklahoma, but now lived in a San Francisco suburb, became caught up in this protest. She was already helping out at her local American Indian center, but she wanted to do more—something really important that would make a difference. The takeover at Alcatraz helped her focus on what she wanted to do.

For the 18 months that the island remained occupied, Mankiller dedicated herself to their cause. She spent most of her time at the San Francisco Indian Center, where she helped to raise money and collected food and clothing for those who chose to stay on the island. She also visited the island several times helping out in whatever way she could.

Being part of the Alcatraz takeover was a crucial turning point in Mankiller's life. She later said, "No matter where my path takes me, I must always remember where the journey started. It was in San Francisco —at Alcatraz." At the time, Wilma Mankiller had no idea that that path would take her back to her Cherokee lands in Oklahoma to become the first woman principal chief of the Cherokee people.

Wilma Pearl Mankiller was born on November 18, 1945, in the Cherokee capital of Tahlequah, Oklahoma. She lived with her father, a full Cherokee, her Dutch-Irish mother, and her 10 brothers and sisters in Mankiller Flats, on a 160-acre farm once owned by Wilma's paternal grandfather.

As a child, Wilma learned the history of her people. She learned that the Cherokee were once hunters who lived in the forests and mountains of the southeastern United States. She learned that the Mankiller name *Asgaya-dih* was once a title honoring the person designated as the official protector of a village. She learned about the Trail of Tears when, in 1839, the United States government ordered thousands of Cherokee to leave their ancestral homes and travel, mostly by foot, to a new Indian Territory more than 1,200 miles away. Thousands of Cherokee died during this long journey. The survivors settled onto their new land and made new lives for themselves as farmers. But their suffering was not over. As white settlers moved further west, they took more and more of the land promised to the Cherokee. In 1907, when Oklahoma became a state, the government took even more Cherokee land. They also took ownership of the land away from the tribe and redistributed it as individual farms. That was when Mankiller Flats was deeded to Wilma's grandfather.

As a young girl, Wilma enjoyed wandering the quiet woods near her home and didn't mind her chore of hauling water from a far distant spring back to the farm—which had no running water or electricity. She may have lived in poverty, but she didn't feel poor because she felt secure in the tribal community where everyone knew and cared about everyone else.

When Wilma was 12 years old, a severe drought in Oklahoma caused crop failures, making the Cherokee even poorer than they had been. The Bureau of Indian Affairs thought the way to solve the problem was to move the Cherokee off their farms and into cities where employment opportunities were supposed to be better. Anyone who agreed to participate in this relocation program was promised help in finding a place to live and a job. Because he was desperate to support his large family, Wilma's father accepted the government's offer and the Mankillers moved to San Francisco.

The move was difficult for Wilma. She hated the noise, traffic, and harshness of city life and missed the fields and woods she had left behind. At school, her white classmates and even some of the teachers made fun of her name. Wilma felt isolated and lonely and missed being part of the tightly knit tribal community. For a time, she lived with her grandmother, who had a farm on the outskirts of the city. However, she eventually settled into her new life and finished high school.

In 1963, she married Hector Hugo Olaya, a wealthy Ecuadorean businessman. Hector provided a comfortable home for his wife, and soon the couple had two daughters. But Wilma felt something was missing from her life. She did volunteer work at the San Francisco Indian Center and enrolled first in Skyline Junior College and later at San Francisco State University, where she studied social work.

It was through her work at the Indian Center that she first became involved with the American Indian Movement (AIM) and the Alcatraz protest. After the protest was over, she continued to do volunteer work with local tribal groups. She also worked as Native American coordinator for the San Francisco public schools.

Wilma was happy with the new directions her life was taking, but her husband was not. The couple separated in 1974 and divorced a year later. Mankiller wanted her daughters to know their Cherokee heritage, so she took them back to Mankiller Flats, where she built a small house.

Partly as a result of protests led by the American Indian Movement and other Native American groups, some important changes had occurred in Oklahoma's Cherokee Nation since Wilma had lived there. Before 1971, the federal government appointed a principal chief. Under a new law, the principal chief was elected by the Cherokee people.

Ross Swimmer, the newly elected principal chief, knew there were many problems among his people. Most of them were poor. Alcohol abuse was widespread. Many young people dropped out of school and were often in trouble with

the law. Those young people who did complete their education often left the Indian community. This left a population
of unskilled and unemployed people, many of whom were
on welfare. Swimmer wanted his people to regain the self-
respect they had once had. He wanted them to be self-support-
ing and not have to depend on the federal government for
help. To accomplish his goals he needed to build up a business
and industrial base within tribal lands so people would not
have to leave the Nation to make a decent living.

When Swimmer met Mankiller and learned of her background in social work and her experience in working with
AIM, he hired her as economic stimulus coordinator for the
Cherokee Nation. Her main duties were to encourage young
people to go to college, then return home and help their
people. She also wrote grants to obtain federal funding for
community projects and social services.

She settled into her new life in Tahlequah and returned to
school to complete her college degree at Flaming Rainbow
University in Stillwell. After she obtained her bachelor's
degree, she enrolled in a master's program at the University
of Arkansas just across the state line.

On November 8, 1979, while driving home from the
university, a car coming from the opposite direction hit
Wilma's car head-on. The driver of the other car, who
ironically turned out to be Mankiller's best friend, was killed
at the scene. Mankiller's injuries were so severe that the
paramedics who arrived at the scene thought she was dead
too, but, luckily, they were able to resuscitate her. Her face
was lacerated, her ribs were broken, and one leg was badly
mangled. It took more than 18 operations to restore her face
and repair her leg.

During her long recuperation, she spent hours talking with
tribal elders and searching within herself. The talks helped
her come to a place of "good mind," which she says, helped
her find a new level of spirituality. She said she learned to let

"I wept tears that came
from deep within the
Cherokee part of me.
They were tears from
my history, from my
tribe's past. They were
Cherokee tears."

—Wilma Mankiller

go of the anger she had felt against the government and against white people and, instead, to look to the future with hope.

She was still recuperating from her multiple surgeries when she noticed a loss of muscle control. "My head wouldn't hold up. My eyes didn't work right," she said. At first she thought she was suffering side effects from the medications she was taking. But when she saw a television program about muscular dystrophy, she realized she was seeing her own symptoms being described. Her doctor confirmed her fears and told her she had a special form of muscular dystrophy, called myasthenia gravis. This disease cannot be cured, but it can be treated. Over the next year, Mankiller underwent corrective surgery and chemotherapy to bring her condition under control.

As soon as she was able, she returned to her work. She wanted to find ways to help Native Americans regain the pride and self-esteem that had once been the hallmarks of her people, but which in modern times seemed to have retreated. Mankiller reasoned that one cause of this was that many Native Americans felt they had no control over their own lives, so she came up with a way to change that.

She tested her ideas in Bell, Oklahoma, a small town that, even in 1981, still had no electricity or running water. Sixty percent of the adults in Bell were unemployed; few teenagers finished high school; and alcoholism, fighting, and domestic violence were common problems.

Mankiller proposed a plan to the people of Bell. She would help them obtain federal grant money for basic supplies and equipment to bring in water and electricity and to rebuild their homes. But they would have to do all the planning and work for the project. Under Mankiller's direction, they laid 16 miles of water pipeline and rebuilt their homes. The Bell Project became a model for rebuilding towns throughout America and brought Mankiller national attention. The project also led to the founding of the Cherokee Nation's Community Development Department, of which Mankiller was director.

In 1983, Ross Swimmer asked Mankiller to run as his deputy chief. Many people within the tribe were opposed to a woman holding such a high office. To overcome this opposition, Mankiller reminded the people that in the old days, women traditionally held high positions within Cherokee culture. When a couple was married, the man went to live with his wife's family, and children took their mother's surname, not their father's. Women helped make the tribe's major decisions and often fought with their men in battle. It was only after the Indians began modeling themselves after white society that women took a secondary place. Mankiller must have been convincing, because she and Swimmer won the election.

In 1985, Ross Swimmer left Oklahoma to take a position at the Bureau of Indian Affairs in Washington, D.C. As deputy, Mankiller moved up to principal chief. Once again, she faced opposition. This time, it was not so much because she was a woman but because many of Swimmer's Republican supporters didn't think they could work with Mankiller, who was a Democrat. Mankiller later said that during her first months in office she felt that her opponents were waiting for her to fail. But once Wilma Mankiller decided to undertake something, she was determined to succeed.

The year after she became chief, Mankiller married Charlie Soap, with whom she had worked on the Bell Project. Soap became one of Mankiller's strongest supporters. He

Principal Chief Wilma Mankiller visiting children at the Mary Etta School in Adair County, Oklahoma, September, 1994 (Courtesy Cherokee Nation, Sammy Still, photographer)

encouraged her to run for reelection in 1987. The race was a tight one. But she won by a slight margin, and became the first woman elected as principal chief of a major tribe.

As principal chief, Mankiller wanted to continue the work Swimmer had begun. Some progress had been made, but there were still severe housing shortages, inadequate health care facilities, high unemployment, and a high dropout rate among high school students. Large amounts of money were needed to work on these problems. Some of the money had come from the federal government, but not enough. Mankiller carried on with Swimmer's program of promoting Cherokee-run business and industry. In 1988, she founded the Cherokee Nation Chamber of Commerce, which oversees a number of small independently owned businesses such as hotels, restaurants, gift shops, garden shops, and others. She also introduced many new programs to improve health care and education.

In 1990, Mankiller's work was interrupted when she lost both kidneys to an inherited disease that she had been fighting for 25 years. Her older brother Donald donated one of his kidneys to save his sister's life. As before, she refused to allow illness to stop her.

In 1991, she ran for her third term as chief. Once again, she faced opposition from several tribal members, some of whom sent delegations to her home to ask her not to run. When that didn't work, they resorted to slashing the tires on her car in their attempts to stop her from running. But tactics like this only strengthened her resolve. With the support and help of her husband and her loyal proponents, she won more than 80 percent of the vote.

Mankiller worked not only for the Cherokee, but for all Native American tribes. In recognition of her

> "We need to really trust our own selves and our own thinking, and not allow others to convince us that our thoughts, ideas and plans and visions aren't valid."
>
> —Wilma Mankiller

contributions, she has been awarded many special honors and honorary degrees. She retired from her position as principal chief in 1995. Since that time she has remained as active as her declining health allows. She also finds time to enjoy her children and grandchildren.

Wilma Mankiller once said that as a youngster, she found no role models for herself in history books and wanted to change that. Certainly, she has accomplished her goal. Her strength and determination in the face of unrelenting personal hardship and her unceasing dedication to her people make her a role model for all young women.

Chronology

November 18, 1945	Wilma Mankiller born in Tahlequah, Oklahoma
1957	Mankiller family moves to San Francisco
1963	Wilma Mankiller marries Hugo Olaya
1964	daughter Felicia born
1966	daughter Gina born
1969	Mankiller assists in Alactraz takeover protest
1975	divorces Olaya
1976	moves to Mankiller Flats, Oklahoma
1977	takes first job for Cherokee Nation
1979	suffers servere injuries in auto accident
1981	initiates Bell Community project
1982	founds Community Development Department
1983	appointed as interim deputy chief
1983	elected deputy chief

1985	elected as principal chief, the first woman to hold this position
1986	marries Charlie Soap
1987	elected to second term as principal chief
1988	establishes Cherokee Nation Chamber of Commerce
1991	Wilma Mankiller elected to third term as principal chief
1993	writes autobiography
1995	retires as principal chief

Further Reading

Glassman, Bruce. *Wilma Mankiller: Chief of the Cherokee Nation.* Woodbridge, Conn.: Blackbirch Press, 1992. This young adult book covers Mankiller's life and career.

Mankiller, Wilma and Michael Wallis. *Mankiller: A Chief and Her People.* New York: St. Martin's Press, 1993. Mankiller's autobiography.

Schwarz, Melissa. *Wilma Mankiller, Principal Chief of the Cherokees.* New York: Chelsea House, 1994. A thorough and readable young adult biography. More in-depth than Glassman.

Simon, Charnan. *Wilma P. Mankiller: Chief of the Cherokees.* Danbury, Conn.: Childrens Press. 1991. General overview for younger readers.

Aung San Suu Kyi at her home, Rangoon, Burma, February, 1996 (Courtesy Leslie Kean, the Burma Project)

Aung San Suu Kyi of Burma

(1945–)

On the morning of July 19, 1989, trucks full of armed soldiers rumbled through the quiet residential neighborhood of Rangoon, Burma, where Aung San Suu Kyi (pronounced Oon San Soo Chee) lived. The street was blocked off. The phone lines to Suu Kyi's house were cut, and a tall barbed wire fence was hastily erected around the perimeter of her property. Soldiers burst into her home and held the occupants at gunpoint.

At the time, Suu Kyi was holding a meeting with her top advisers, who were promptly dragged off to prison. Suu Kyi was not. Instead, she was placed under house arrest. No one could enter the house without permission and Suu Kyi could not leave. She was not allowed to communicate with anyone outside the house. Her only crime had been to dare to speak out against the military dictatorship that ruled Burma.

Suu Kyi would be held prisoner for six years. When she was finally released, she told the large crowd of supporters who gathered outside her home, "We're nowhere near democracy. I've been released, that's all."

She was right. Though she repeatedly called for meetings with the government, they refused to speak with her. Their harassment of her and her supporters continued. History seemed to be repeating itself.

Once again, Suu Kyi made speeches calling for free elections and for an end to government violence. She was allowed to speak freely for a little more than a year. Then, in December 1996, the government put a stop to the rallies. Hundreds of her supporters were arrested. In February, 1997, further restrictions were placed on Suu Kyi.

Aung San Suu Kyi was born in Rangoon, Burma, on June 19, 1945. Burma is a land of exotic beauty in the heart of Southeast Asia lying between India, China, and the Indian Ocean. Thousands of gilded pagodas shimmer atop towering mountain peaks like fairy castles in a never-never land. The pagodas are not fairy castles—they are home to orange-robed Buddhist monks. Although Buddhism in a religion that emphasizes peace and tranquillity, Burma is no paradise. Throughout its long history, Burma's people have been ruled by a succession of oppressive rulers.

When Suu Kyi was born, Burma was a British colony that had been invaded by Japan. Suu Kyi's father, General Aung San, worked with the British to helped defeat Japan, then fought against Britain to free his country from colonial rule. Unfortunately Aung San never lived to enjoy the freedom for which he fought. General Aung San was assassinated before Burma's independence in July 1947.

At the time of her father's death, Suu Kyi was only two years old, but her memories of him were kept alive by her mother, Khin Kyi, who conducted a memorial to him each month at the Buddhist shrine in their home, and by the Burmese people, who revered him as a great hero.

When Suu Kyi was 15, her mother was appointed Burma's ambassador to India, and the family moved to Delhi. Jawaharlal Nehru, India's prime minister and a personal friend of Suu Kyi's mother, taught Suu Kyi about Mohandas Gandhi and his philosophy of nonviolent civil disobedience. While Suu Kyi learned about Gandhi and his fight for democracy for India, democracy in Burma came to an abrupt end when General Ne Win seized control of the government.

At 19, Suu Kyi left Asia to attend Oxford University in England, where she studied political science and economics. She was a serious, quiet young woman who dressed in her Burmese *lungyis* (a type of sarong) and who always wore a fresh flower pinned into her ponytail, a practice she continues to this day.

After Suu Kyi earned her degree from Oxford in 1968, she took a position with the United Nations in New York City for three years. In her spare time, she did volunteer work at a hospital, took a bus trip across America, and wrote long letters to her fiancé, Michael Aris, a British student she had met at Oxford.

Perhaps she had a premonition of what the future would hold for her because before she agreed to marry Michael, she wrote to him, "I only ask one thing: that should my people need me, you would help me do my duty by them." Michael, a student of Asian civilization, agreed, and they were married in a Buddhist ceremony in 1972.

The couple spent the first year of their marriage in Bhutan, a kingdom high in the Himalayan Mountains, where Michael tutored the royal children and Suu Kyi worked for the foreign ministry. After that, they returned to England. Michael taught at Oxford University and Suu Kyi gave birth to their first son, Alexander. A second son, Kim, was born in 1977. During these years, Suu Kyi wrote a biography of her father, enrolled in a graduate studies program in Burmese literature, and wrote a children's book, entitled *Let's Visit Burma.*

In March 1988, Suu Kyi received a telephone call from Burma informing her that her mother had had a stroke. Suu Kyi flew to Burma and was caught up in events that would catapult her to world fame.

Each day on her way in and out of the hospital where her mother lay dying, she passed crowds of students protesting the increasing brutality and repressiveness of Ne Win's government. Although the students were unarmed, the police often used gunfire to disperse them. By June, several hundred students had been killed and thousands had been sent to prisons where they were subject to torture.

The protests spread to every major city in Burma. Factory workers, businesspeople, doctors, teachers, housewives—even monks who usually stayed out of politics—joined the demonstrations. The government's reaction was more brutality. Suu Kyi sympathized with the protesters but felt her first priority was her mother.

Burma's government was in turmoil. General Ne Win announced his retirement and promised a special election for the people to choose a new government. The election never took place. Instead, an associate of Ne Win's was appointed chairman, but Ne Win remained in control.

Suu Kyi, who remembered her father and his dream of democracy for Burma, felt it was time for the people to take action. But she also remembered the lessons she had learned about Gandhi. She sent messages to the protesters urging them to continue to call for democracy but through only nonviolent methods of protest.

Shwedagon Pagoda, where Aung San Suu Kyi first spoke to the people of Burma (Courtesy Larry Dohrs)

During one week in August 1988, more than 3,000 protesters were killed. Suu Kyi wrote a letter to the Council of State demanding an end to the brutality. Her letter was ignored. She felt she had to do something more. Her friends warned her not to become involved. "I can't help it," she said, "I have already decided, and I have to sacrifice my personal life to the limit."

Two days later more than 500,000 people gathered in front of the Shwedagon Pagoda. They carried posters painted with General Aung San's portrait above their heads and waited to hear his daughter speak. After calling for a moment of silence to honor those who had been killed, Suu Kyi quoted her father's words: "'We must make democracy the popular creed. . . . If we should fail to do this, our people are bound to suffer. . . .' That is what my father said. It is the reason why I am participating in this struggle." She demanded an end to the one-party system and fair and free elections.

In September, a small group of military leaders calling themselves the State Law and Order Restoration Council (SLORC) took over the government. They promised to allow the formation of new political parties and free elections—sometime.

Suu Kyi and her followers established the National League for Democracy (NLD) and Suu Kyi was elected general secretary, but nothing changed. There were no

"You should not let your fears prevent you from doing what you know is right. Not that you shouldn't be afraid. Fear is normal. But to be inhibited from doing what you know is right, that is what is dangerous. You should be able to lead your life in the right way—despite your fears."

—Aung San Suu Kyi

elections. Suu Kyi continued to speak out. She traveled throughout the country speaking in cities, towns, and villages.

Once, Suu Kyi and her advisers were confronted by six soldiers who had been ordered to shoot her. When the soldiers crouched in firing position, Suu Kyi stepped away from her companions and walked up to the soldiers, silently daring them to shoot. The soldiers lowered their guns. Asked why she had taken such a risk, she said, "It seemed so much simpler to provide them with a single target than to bring everyone else in."

In an attempt to stop Suu Kyi from speaking to large crowds, the government prohibited political gatherings of more than four people. Suu Kyi defied the laws and continued to speak to the thousands of people who gathered to hear her. When the police prevented her from making speeches, she made tapes and videos that her supporters distributed among the people.

Unable to stop her any other way, the government placed Suu Kyi under house arrest. When the soldiers took her advisers to prison, Suu Kyi was afraid they would be tortured. In an attempt to prevent this, she went on a hunger strike for 12 days, refusing to ingest anything other than water. This was not her only act of defiance. She found ways to frustrate her captors throughout her imprisonment.

At the time she was arrested, Suu Kyi's sons were visiting from England. Within a few days, her husband arrived. The three of them were allowed to stay with her for several weeks. Then Michael and the boys had to return to England. Suu Kyi could have gone with them—if she agreed to leave Burma and not return. She refused. She did not know she would not see her children again for more than two years.

"It is not enough to simply 'live and let live.' Genuine tolerance requires an active effort to try to understand the point of view of others."

—Aung San Suu Kyi

In May 1990, the government thought that with Suu Kyi unable to rally her people, the NLD would break into too many factions to gain a majority of votes, so they finally held the long-promised elections. The government made a bad miscalculation. Although neither Suu Kyi nor her top advisers were able to participate in the campaign, their NLD won more than 80 percent of the vote. The government ignored the results of the election and carried on with its military rule.

While she was held in isolation, Suu Kyi maintained her sanity by following a strict daily routine. Each morning she exercised, then spent time meditating. She kept herself informed about the outside world by listening to news reports on the radio. She read books on many subjects, but especially enjoyed reading biographies of other dissidents. She later said that reading those biographies gave her the strength to persevere. She also wrote a number of essays, which she was able to smuggle to her husband in England. She stated that her time alone helped her to learn patience and to control her flaring temper.

Suu Kyi may have been unable to speak to the world during her years of house arrest, but her husband and supporters kept her name and her cause alive. Michael assembled her letters and transcripts of some of her speeches into a book titled *Freedom from Fear*. Burma's government was condemned by the United Nations, Amnesty International (a worldwide organization dedicated to freedom for political prisoners), and by free countries around the world.

All called for her release and for economic sanctions against Burma.

In 1991, Suu Kyi was awarded the Nobel Peace Prize in recognition of her struggle to bring freedom to Burma. Her captors said she could go to Oslo to accept her award—if she agreed not to return to Burma. She turned down the offer. Her husband and sons accepted the award for her. The offer of freedom was made several times, but always under the condition that Suu Kyi leave Burma permanently. Each time the offer was made, Suu Kyi refused.

Aung San Suu Kyi's birthday and "Children's Day," February 13, 1996
(Courtesy Leslie Kean, the Burma Project)

In the early 1990s, Burma's government was trying to build the country's economy. They sought investments from foreign governments and companies. They also wanted to promote tourism to Burma. But the bad publicity they were getting from Amnesty International and the United Nations interfered with this. In an attempt to look better to the outside world, the government freed Suu Kyi in July 1995.

For several months after her release, the government watched but did not interfere with the weekly rallies she held outside her home. Continuing her dedication to nonviolence and determined to establish a spirit of cooperation, she advised people to have patience and to try and work with the government. She repeatedly asked to meet with government officials. But the government didn't respond to her overtures.

By the fall of 1996, Suu Kyi and her followers were being harassed just as they had been before her imprisonment. Aside from supporting mobs of hecklers paid to attack her and her party as they traveled to and from meetings, the government again barricaded her street and home and finally stopped her weekly meetings. Suu Kyi knew she might be arrested again or assassinated. "There's not much point in worrying about it," she told a reporter, "I know I'm going to die one day."

As of early 1998, Burma was still ruled by SLORC. Aung San Suu Kyi and other members of the NLD were still being persecuted by the government. Thousands of political prisoners languished in prisons where they were subjected to terrible conditions and torture. United Nations advisers were consistently refused access to these prisons.

Suu Kyi is not allowed to speak with reporters or hold any public meetings. Her movements are so severely restricted that she is once again effectively under house arrest. Amnesty International, the Free Burma Coalition, and several other organizations continue their efforts to free Burma from oppression. Through these organizations, Suu Kyi appeals to students in America and the rest of the free world to support her efforts to bring freedom to Burma. Major corporations with investments in Burma have been urged to withdraw, and other corporations are urged not to invest in Burma.

Aung San Suu Kyi's name means "a bright collection of strange victories." With her indomitable spirit, she has already won many strange victories. She has also won the hearts of people across the world who draw inspiration from her.

Chronology

June 19, 1945	Aung San Suu Kyi is born in Rangoon, Burma
1947	her father, General Aung San, is assassinated
1948	Burma freed from English colonial rule
1960	Suu Kyi moves to India with mother
1962	Ne Win takes over Burma as military dictator
1964	Suu Kyi enters Oxford University
1972	marries Michael Aris
1973	son Alexander is born
1977	son Kim is born
March 1988	Suu Kyi leaves England to go to Burma to visit her mother
August 1988	makes her first public speech
September 1988	helps found National League for Democracy; elected general secretary

December 1988	her mother, Khin Kyi, dies
July 10, 1989	Suu Kyi is placed under house arrest; prohibited from speaking to the people of Burma
1990	awarded Thorolf Rafto Memorial Prize for Human Rights
1990	NLD wins general election
1990	Suu Kyi awarded Sakharov Prize for Freedom of Thought
1991	awarded Nobel Peace Prize
July 1995	freed from house arrest
1996	holds weekly meetings with supporters
December 1996	again prohibited from speaking to the people of Burma
February 1998	held under partial house arrest; actions severely restricted by government

Further Reading

Ghosh, Amitav. "A Reporter at Large: Burma." *The New Yorker*, August 12, 1996. An examination of Burma's history since its independence. Also covers Suu Kyi in depth.

Parenteau, John. *Prisoner for Peace: Aung San Suu Kyi and Burma's Struggle for Democracy.* Greensboro, N.C.: Morgan Reynolds, Inc., 1994. Excellent young adult biography.

Stewart, Whitney. *Aung San Suu Kyi: Fearless Voice of Burma.* Minneapolis, Minn.: Lerner Publications, 1997. A young adult biography tracing Aung San Suu Kyi's lifelong dedication to restoring freedom to her country.

Suu Kyi, Aung San. *Freedom From Fear and Other Writings.* Edited by Michael Aris. London: Viking, 1991. Collection of writings by and about Aung San Suu Kyi.

————. *Let's Visit Burma*. London: Burket Publishing, 1985. Provides good historical and background information. Of interest because Suu Kyi is author.

Wallenchinsky, David "How One Woman Became the Voice of Her People." *Parade*, January 19, 1997. Excellent in-depth profile

Yin, Saw Myat. *Burma* (Cultures of the World Series). New York: Marshall Cavendish, 1990. Brief mention of Suu Kyi.

Benazir Bhutto was prime minister of Pakistan, first in 1988 and again in 1993. Both times she was forced out of office before the end of her term.
(Courtesy Embassy of Pakistan)

Benazir Bhutto of Pakistan

(1 9 5 3 –   )

"**I**t is cold. I hear the prison clock strike one o'clock, then two o'clock. I can't sleep. The chill desert wind sweeps through the open bars of my cell . . . a huge cage, an enormous space with only a rope cot in it. I twist and turn on the cot, my teeth chattering. I have no sweater, no blanket, nothing. Only the shalwar khameez [a typical Pakistani style dress] I had been wearing when I was arrested. One of the jailers had felt sorry for me and (quietly) passed me a pair of socks. But she was so frightened of being caught for her charity that this morning she had asked for them back. My bones ache. If only I could see, I could at least walk around. But the electricity is turned off in my cell at night. From seven o'clock on, there is nothing but the cold darkness." This is how Benazir Bhutto described her first days of what turned out to be five months of solitary confinement in 1981.

Bhutto, the daughter of Pakistan's former prime minister, was considered an enemy of Pakistan's military government from the moment her father's government had been toppled in 1977. For seven years, she was repeatedly held under house arrest, jailed, or exiled.

In 1988, Benazir Bhutto was elected prime minister of Pakistan. She was the first woman ever to head a modern Muslim country and one of the youngest heads of state in the world. She was loved by many of her own people and hailed around the globe as Pakistan's hope for democracy. Since then, she has become one of the most controversial politicians in the world. Her first term of office ended in 1990 when she was accused of misconduct and corruption. The charges were never proved. In 1993, she was reelected as prime minister— but was once again charged with corruption and forced out of office in 1996.

Mohtarma Benazir Bhutto was born on June 21, 1953, in Karachi, Pakistan. Nicknamed Pinky because of her fair complexion, she was the oldest of four children of Zulfikar Ali Bhutto and Nusrat Ispahani Bhutto, one of Pakistan's wealthiest and most prominent families.

Most Pakistanis are Muslims, followers of the religion of Islam. Many Muslims believe women must follow the customs of purdah—that is, they must dress in long, dark clothing and always hide their faces behind a veil; they must never speak to a man who is not related to them; and they must be totally subservient to all men. Though the Bhutto family followed the Muslim faith, they did not follow purdah. Like her mother before her, Benazir was brought up with much greater freedom than most Pakistani girls. She received a first-rate education and, from the time she was very young, was encouraged to think for herself and speak her mind.

As a very young child, her teacher was her English governess. Later, she attended a Catholic school because of its excellent academic program. She did not take part in the

Benazir Bhutto speaking at Harvard University (Courtesy Harvard University News Office)

school's religious instruction and continued to practice her own religion. When she was 16, she left Pakistan to attend Radcliffe College in the United States.

Life in the United States was very different from anything Benazir had known in Pakistan. At home, she was used to servants who drove her everywhere she needed to go and who took care of her every need. She was also used to living in a Muslim world where behavior was very restrained—especially for girls.

When she first came to America, she was amazed at the way students talked back to their professors and parents, the open and casual relationships between boys and girls, and the freedom enjoyed by women. But she adjusted quickly and it wasn't long before she was taking part in anti–Vietnam War protests and women's rights marches.

While Benazir was in the United States, there was a civil war raging in Pakistan. When that war ended, her father, who was the head of the People's Party, became his country's first elected prime minister. Benazir was thrilled with her father's victory and looked forward to working with his administration when she finished school.

She graduated from Radcliffe in 1973 and continued her studies at Oxford University in England, where she majored in political science, economics, and diplomacy. She joined the debating club and was elected its president—the first non-English woman to be so honored.

She received her degree from Oxford in 1977 and returned home where she was assigned a minor government post. But within days of her arrival, her father's government was overthrown by General Mohammed Zia al-Haq. Bhutto's father was arrested for "crimes against the state" and thrown into prison.

Bhutto and her mother became co-leaders of the People's Party. They demanded Ali's release and a return to an elected government. One time when Bhutto visited her father in prison, he told her, "My daughter, should anything happen to me, you will continue my mission." When he was hanged in 1979, Bhutto vowed to clear his name and to restore the People's Party to power. Bhutto was arrested and jailed several times for opposing the dictatorship that had ousted her father's government. During one of her imprisonments she suffered a serious ear injury, and in 1984 she was allowed to travel to England for medical treatment. While she was there, one of her two brothers, Shahnawaz, who at the time was living in Paris, was poisoned. Bhutto brought his body back to Pakistan to be buried. She made speeches accusing Zia's government of murdering her brother. Because of this, she was exiled from the country. She returned to England, where she continued to speak out against Pakistan's military rulers to the Western world. Meanwhile, her mother continued to speak out against the government at home.

In 1986, Bhutto was allowed to return to Pakistan. When she arrived, she was greeted at the airport by tens of thousands of supporters who cheered her as their leader. For the next two years she and her mother campaigned and worked to rebuild the People's Party.

Bhutto knew that as a woman leader in a Muslim country, she had to be very careful not to appear to be too "Westernized." She dressed in traditional Pakistani clothing, and while she did not wear a veil, she did keep her head covered with a scarf. She also thought she would receive more support from conservative Pakistanis if she were married and had children. For this reason, she agreed to an arranged marriage (which is traditional and still common in Pakistan) to Asif Zardari,

"Power is no big deal. What is more important is that the people always have respect for you."

—Benazir Bhutto

who like her, was a member of one of Pakistan's wealthiest families. She later said that although she did not know her husband before they married, they soon came to love one another—just as her mother had predicted. The following year she had the first of her four children. Within days of his birth, she was back on the campaign trail. Though Zia had promised free elections, no one in Pakistan really thought this would happen.

But then, in the summer of 1988, Zia was killed in a plane crash. That fall elections were held, and in December Bhutto was elected prime minister. Once in office, she tried to restore the country to democracy. She lifted restrictions against the press and freed many people who had been jailed without trial. She tried but was not able to start new social service programs to help the vast numbers of people in her country who lived in extreme poverty. She also tried to improve conditions for women in her country.

Although there were always a small number of Pakistani women, who like Bhutto, were well-educated and who enjoyed freedom in their personal lives, most Pakistani women lived under conditions the Western world considers primitive. Husbands were free to beat and even kill their wives without fear of punishment. If a woman accused a man of rape, she had to have four male witnesses to prove her claim. And if a woman became pregnant as a result of rape, she was often jailed and publicly beaten for having had sex with a man who was not her husband. A woman could vote only if she had a card saying she had her husband's permission to do so. The plight of children was almost as bad as that of women. Education was not mandatory, and hundreds of thousands of young children were sent out to work in factories or farms instead of going to school. Some of this was due to Muslim fundamentalists, who opposed change and supported a literal interpretation of Islamic scriptures.

Prime minister Benazir Bhutto unveils plaque at groundbreaking ceremony of 5280 MG power station at Keti Bandar. (Courtesy Embassy of Pakistan)

Many people had hoped that Bhutto would be able to change these things, but because she was forced to work with a fundamentalist Muslim majority, she was limited in what she could do. But in spite of these difficulties, she was able to set up a number of health care and legal aid centers. She also appointed a number of women judges, hired women police officers, and even established police stations staffed entirely by women as places of refuge to which abused women could go without fear of being immediately returned to their husbands.

Political power in Pakistan has always been complicated by ongoing rivalries between the president, the military, and the prime minister. In 1990, after only two years in office,

Bhutto was fired from her position as prime minister by Ghulam Ishaq Kahn, the president of the country, who claimed she had misused government funds and was running a corrupt administration. Bhutto attempted to regain her position in a hastily called election but was not successful. She did, however, keep her Parliament seat. Then, in 1993, she was reelected when Nawaz Sharif, the man who had replaced her, was himself dismissed for corruption.

Her second term was as full of problems as her first. Not only did she have to contend with several opposing parties, but she faced opposition from within her own party and her own family. Her surviving brother Murtaza returned to Pakistan after 10 years of exile and claimed that he, not she, was the rightful heir to their father, Ali Bhutto. Benazir's mother, who had previously worked with her daughter, switched her allegiance to her son.

Bhutto's political troubles grew worse when her brother was assassinated by police who claimed he was resisting arrest. Bhutto claimed that her political enemies had arranged for the shooting so they could blame her. Those who were opposed to Bhutto claimed she and her husband were behind the killing. Once again, she was embroiled in accusations of improper behavior, mishandling of financial matters, and corruption.

In November 1996, Bhutto was fired for the second time by the president. Both she and her husband were jailed. She was freed within a few days, but her husband remained incarcerated on charges of complicity in the murder of Bhutto's brother Murtaza.

"Life is not always fair, it is not always just, but even if it is not fair, and even if it is not just, it is important to go on working for what you believe in."

—Benazir Bhutto

New elections were scheduled for February 1997. Bhutto vowed she would triumph yet again at the polls, but this time she was wrong. She lost the election to Nawaz Sharif, the man whom she had replaced in 1993.

Making as assessment of a political figure as currently controversial as Benazir Bhutto is difficult. After the election in 1996, many people still regarded Bhutto as a hero of freedom and democracy. Others claimed she had been corrupted by power. Still others thought she was always corrupt, and that her father had also been corrupt. In January 1998 the corruption charges against Bhutto and her husband widened. Papers and documents obtained by the government and the press show details of more than $100 million deposited in foreign banks and properties purchased by Bhutto's husband during the years she was in office. Bhutto denied the charges and said they were politically motivated by the current prime minister who wanted to discredit her to prevent her from seeking public office in the future. But the facts remain that during her five years in office, Pakistan's treasury was drained and she was unable to put into place many of the programs she had promised. When she left office, Pakistan was more than $62 billion in debt. In spite of the charges against her and the ongoing investigation, Bhutto maintains her position as leader of Pakistan's major opposition party, the Pakistan People's Party. As with other politicians of present times, it will remain for future generations to truly assess their accomplishments—and whether they were heroes or villains.

Chronology

| June 21, 1953 | Benazir Bhutto born in Karachi, Pakistan |
| 1969 | enters Radcliffe |

1971	Bhutto's father, Zulfikar Ali Bhutto, elected prime minister
1973	Benazir Bhutto graduates from Radcliffe College; attends Oxford University
1976	graduates from Oxford and extends studies one year
1977	returns to Pakistan; a military coup ousts Ali Bhutto; Benazir Bhutto jailed numerous times
1977–84	Zia al-Haq rules Pakistan; Benazir Bhutto jailed again
1979	Ali Bhutto hanged
1984	goes to England
1985	her brother Shahnawaz is poisoned in Paris; Bhutto returns to Pakistan, is arrested and exiled
December 18, 1987	Bhutto marries Asif Ali Zardari
1988	gives birth to first son
1988	elected as prime minister
1993	Prime Minister Mian Nawaz Sharif is accused of corruption; Sharif and President Ishaq Kahn resign; Parliament is dissolved
	Bhutto's is reelected for second term as prime minister
September 1996	brother Murtaza is killed
November 1996	Bhutto fired for second time on charges of corruption; her husband, Ali Zardari, is jailed
February 3, 1997	Bhutto loses election for third term as prime minister
January 1998	New charges of corruption leveled against Bhutto and her husband

Further Reading

Bhutto, Benazir. *Daughter of Destiny*: New York: Simon & Schuster, 1989. Her autobiography.

Bouchard, Elizabeth. *Benazir Bhutto: Prime Minister*. Woodbridge, Conn.: Blackbirch Press, 1992. A biography for younger readers.

Doherty, Katherine M. and Craig A. Doherty. *Benazir Bhutto*. Danbury, Conn.: Franklin Watts, 1990. Thoroughly researched account of Bhutto's life until 1990. For young adults.

Hughes, Libby. *Benazir Bhutto: From Prison to Prime Minister*. Morristown, New Jersey: Dillon Press, 1990. A readable biography with a note by Bhutto.

Liswood, Laura A. *Women World Leaders*. New York: HarperCollins, 1995. An excellent book containing short biographies, interviews, and evaluations of several women heads of state.

Index